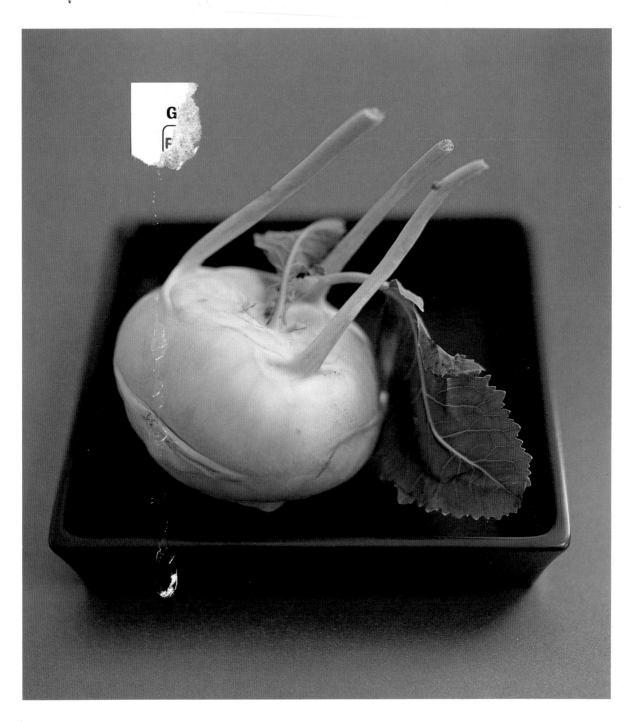

Vegetables

The new food heroes

Peter Gordon

Quadrille

Photography by Jean Cazals

This book is dedicated to my gran, Molly Gordon, who was the best vegetable grower ever – although my dad, Bruce, is pretty good too.

All recipes in the book serve 4 as a main course unless otherwise stated.

First published in 2006 by
Quadrille Publishing Limited,
Alhambra House,
27–31 Charing Cross Road,
London WC2H 0LS

Paperback edition published in 2007

Editorial Director: Jane O'Shea
Creative Director: Helen Lewis
Editor & Project Manager: Lewis Esson
Art Direction & Design: Lawrence Morton
Photography: Jean Cazals
Food Styling: Peter Gordon
Styling: Sue Rowlands
Production: Bridget Fish, Vincent Smith

Cataloguing in Publication Data: a catalogue record for this book is available from the British Library

ISBN-13: 978 184400 514 7

Printed and bound in China

introduction

Vegetables are often the unsung heroes of a meal. They support the main protagonist, usually a meat or fish component, but without them said protagonist would be on the stage alone. No supporting cast, no one to bounce off, no one to talk to, no one to fill the stage when they need a break. Once the meat (or fish) has gone – what's left?

At The Providores and Tapa Room, our restaurant in London, and also at dine by Peter Gordon, my restaurant in New Zealand, we treat vegetables with the highest respect. In fact, it is often the vegetable that determines the final nature of the main course dish. In spring and summer, there is a plethora of ingredients to choose from, but in the cooler months it tends to be the hard root vegetables that we have to be more inventive with, as well as the brassicas that benefit from frost (cavolo nero, Brussels sprouts) and the onion family – laid down since late summer.

For vegetarians, of course, this may seem a little over the top, but for those of us who like to eat flesh with our meals, the vegetable needs to be given a new-found respect and proper recognition. In this book, the recipes are primarily vegetarian main courses, but they can also be served in smaller portions as side dishes, or as accompaniments to the aforementioned protein. Inside, you'll find fritters, soups, salads, casseroles and curries, wok- and deep-fried dishes, roasts, gratins, bakes and braises, pies, tarts, frittatas and quiches, noodles and rice-based dishes, and pickles and preserves. Plus, there are even a few vegetable-based desserts.

As the world becomes more switched on to exotic vegetables (bitter melons, plantains, kumara, etc), while also appreciating regional ones (heirloom potatoes and tomatoes, autumn squash, etc), the shopper is now able to use and experiment with an exciting array of vegetables. Make for a farmers' market to see what's regional and locally sourced, or head to your nearest ethnic food store – and even some of the larger supermarkets – to see what's being cooked in your neighbourhood and that you're probably not too familiar with.

Properly grown vegetables are healthy – and by that, I mean vegetables that have been grown with little or no pesticides or phosphates. As part of a balanced diet, they'll keep your body in fine form and your mind equally athletic. Vegetables play a major part in almost every diet and they are used in numerous ways, depending on the regime; from the raw food diet through to the juice diet, they'll be there looking after your body's needs.

When buying vegetables, however, you need to be aware of what is fresh and what is past its best. If you're in a position to handle the vegetables, then you're off to a good start – although in some shops they wrap everything so tightly in plastic that you'd have to open the packets to check it. Vegetables are mostly made up of water – much like us humans – and, when they are young and healthy, they will be firmly plump, hard, vividly coloured and turgid. A firm, crisp, dense vegetable is ideal.

Courgettes and marrows should be almost bursting from their skins. A limp bean or asparagus spear is a thing of sadness – well past its prime. If you're able to bend them backwards and they snap with a clean sound, then you have very fresh examples; if they bend flexibly, then don't bother with them. Broccoli and cauliflower should have tight florets, not flaccid ones that are beginning to flower – a sure sign they're way past it. Squash and pumpkins need to sound hollow when you tap them and need to be heavy – although there are some pumpkins that are mostly a thin layer of flesh surrounding a hollow centre, but these tend to have little flavour, so I'd avoid them anyway. Potatoes should be neither green-skinned nor sprouting. While you can pick the sprouting eyes off, the skin tends to give the potato a metallic flavour. Wild mushrooms can sometimes be full of worm-like insects – while these won't kill you, they don't look so great. The best way to see if your mushrooms have these is to split the stalks across and lengthways – you'll soon see any unwanted creatures.

When storing vegetables, cool and dark are best. Bright sun and too much warmth are the enemies of vegetables once they've been pulled from the earth – they may like it when growing but not after. You don't need to keep veggies in the fridge, except in the height of summer, but remember that as a fridge chills your food it is also desiccating it. So when storing vegetables in the fridge make sure they're kept in a plastic bag with a little hole in it, if you don't have a special vegetable compartment in yours.

Mushrooms, especially wild ones, can sometimes go slimy if kept too long in the fridge, so try to eat them as soon as you can after buying them – you can even clean them and cook them, then eat them a few days later. Never keep potatoes in the fridge, as they tend to soften; just store them in a paper bag in a cool dark place, such as a kitchen cupboard. Bearing all this advice in mind, you may prefer to avoid buying your vegetables from shops that display their produce in the sun-drenched window or on the pavement.

But if you can't, take them home and give them a soak in cold water, pat them dry and place them in the fridge to crisp up.

Regarding preparation of vegetables, the nature of their upbringing will determine how you treat them once home. Organic vegetables will have no pesticides used on them, so the whole thing – skin, stalks and all – can be eaten. Vegetables grown with the assistance of sprays and pesticides will always need peeling or scrubbing – especially root vegetables. I wash any vegetable before cooking it – more often than not, it will have picked up dust and dirt from being transported from field to shop, and that's not what I like to eat. Wild mushrooms need to have all the twigs and grit removed from them (a laborious job but worthwhile), and a firm pastry brush is ideal for this. They will absorb water very easily, so if you get fed up trying to clean them and dirt still sticks, plunge them into a bowl of cold water, swirl it around for 10 seconds, count to 5, then pull them out and drain in a colander (don't pour them and the water into a colander as all the bits will end up on top of them). Pat them dry between layers of absorbent kitchen paper or a cloth, then cook immediately, or they can go slimy and begin to lose their flavour.

When it comes to onions and the tears they evoke, there are many suggested ways to avoid this, but here is mine. Place them in the fridge an hour or two before you're going to prepare them. Cut the stalk end off, keeping the root end intact, and peel the skin off by cutting vertically through the papery layer and pulling it off. If you breathe through your mouth, not your nose, you are less likely to weep. An easy way to do this is to hold a toothpick between your front teeth – it keeps you breathing properly. I've also heard it said that wearing sunglasses helps!

To peel a lot of garlic, break the head into individual cloves and pour on plenty of tepid water, then leave for 6 hours. When the time comes to peel them, the skin will slip off much more easily. If your garlic has a green shoot inside, then it's wise to cut it vertically and pick the shoot out – otherwise it will taste a little bitter and give you wind.

Enjoy your greens... and reds, and other coloured vegetables – and remember they are not just lovely flavours and textures to cook and eat, they can do you the world of good and they will enhance any meal.

soups

Chilled tomato, red pepper and chilli soup

This is a relatively simple-to-make summer soup (although, funnily enough, it's also quite good served hot in winter). You can make it as spicy as you want, with more or less chilli; and for another flavour dimension, replace the chilli altogether with *pimentón* (Spanish smoked paprika), or use a tin of piquillo peppers in place of the red peppers for a light smoky taste.

5 tablespoons extra-virgin olive oil, plus more for drizzling

2 red onions, thinly sliced

2 garlic cloves, chopped

½–1 red chilli (you can make it as chilli hot, or not, as you want)

3 red peppers, halved, deseeded and roughly chopped

2 tablespoons sherry vinegar (or use a good red wine vinegar, or even just straight sherry with a squeeze of lemon juice)

700g ripe tomatoes, roughly chopped (or 600g tinned chopped tomatoes)

1 egg

1 spring onion, thinly sliced

Heat a wide pan, add the oil, then after a second or two add the onions, garlic and chilli, and cook over a high heat, stirring often, to caramelize the onions.

Add the peppers and continue cooking for another few minutes. Add the vinegar and tomatoes, mix well, then add 200ml water and bring to the boil. Cover and simmer for 20 minutes. If the heat is too low, the vegetables won't soften enough, so make sure it's at a rapid simmer (or a very gentle boil).

Once the soup is cooked, purée it (try using a stick blender or goblet blender with the lid loosely on – a food processor isn't the best for hot liquids). You can pass it through a sieve, but it's not necessary.

Tip it into a wide dish, add salt to taste, then cover with a sheet of baking parchment and allow to cool to room temperature. Place in the fridge and leave to go completely cold.

Meanwhile, boil the egg for 5 minutes, then refresh under cold running water. Shell and either grate or chop the egg.

To serve, give the soup a stir, adjust the seasoning, then ladle it into 4 bowls. Place some egg and spring onions on top, then drizzle with some more extra-virgin olive oil.

serves 4–6

¼ cauliflower

60g butter

7 tablespoons extra-virgin olive oil

1 teaspoon cumin seeds

1 medium leek, sliced and well rinsed to remove any grit

3 garlic cloves, peeled

1 large sweet potato (about 400g), peeled and cut into chunks

1 bay leaf, torn in half

2 pinches of saffron

1.2 litres vegetable stock

1 large slice of stale bread, crusts removed and the bread cut into cubes

chopped chives for garnish

Sweet potato, leek, cumin, saffron and cauliflower soup

This soup is very earthy in its flavours, with the saffron also adding a lovely hue to it and the croutons providing texture. By frying the cauliflower, as opposed to the more usual steaming or boiling, you get totally unexpected characteristics from the vegetable – it becomes sweet, mild and crunchy.

Remove the thick stalks from the cauliflower and roughly chop the florets into pieces. Heat a large pot, add half the butter and let it cook to a light nut-brown. Add 2 tablespoons of the olive oil, then add the cauliflower and cook over a moderate-to-high heat to caramelize it, stirring often. Tip the cauliflower into a bowl and wipe out the pot.

Return the pot to the heat, add the remaining butter with the cumin and again cook the butter to a light nut-brown colour. Add 2 tablespoons of the olive oil, then add the leek and 2 of the garlic cloves, which you have roughly chopped, and sauté until the leek has wilted.

Add the sweet potato, bay leaf, saffron and vegetable stock, and bring to the boil. Turn down to a rapid simmer and cook until the potato is tender, then adjust the seasoning.

While the soup is cooking, make the croutons: smash the remaining garlic clove with the side of a large knife and place in a small pan with the remaining 3 tablespoons of olive oil. Place over a medium heat, add the cubed bread and cook until the bread turns golden, stirring constantly to prevent it and the garlic from burning. Once they are ready, tip the croutons and oil into a bowl, discarding the cooked garlic bits.

To serve, ladle the soup into bowls, spoon some cauliflower on top, then scatter with the croutons, together with the oil in which they were cooked and some chives.

Shiitake ginger broth with seaweed

This soup is by no means hearty, but it is very satisfying. It is Japanese in origin, and you can use the basic broth as a starting point for many variations on the theme. Try adding diced tofu or a little miso, sliced cooked chicken or duck, cooked and shelled prawns or crab meat, cooked noodles or even shaved vegetables. You needn't head to a Japanese supermarket or Chinatown to source the seaweed and dried shiitake, as these can often be bought from health-food shops. Shiitake mushrooms come in many sizes and grades – here I used small Japanese ones the size of a 50p coin – if you find yourself with larger ones, then use a few less. For the seaweed, I use dried kombu (which works rather like a stock cube) and dried mixed sea vegetables.

16cm piece of dried kombu

16 small dried shiitake mushrooms (or use 10 large ones)

12 fresh shiitake mushrooms

2 thumbs of ginger

6cm piece of leek

very small handful of dried mixed seaweed (sometimes called sea vegetables)

4 tablespoons mirin

125ml soy sauce (Japanese soy sauce will work better than Chinese in this dish)

4 teaspoons toasted sesame oil

Rinse the kombu under cool running water for 20 seconds, rubbing it gently, then pat dry with a cloth and place in a saucepan with 1.2 litres of cold water.

Place the dried shiitake in a bowl of tepid water and mix them around with your hand for 30 seconds to dislodge any grit. Leave them for a minute, then add to the saucepan with the kombu, discarding the soaking water.

Break or cut the stalks from the fresh shiitake and add these to the pan, then slice the caps thinly and set aside. Peel all the ginger; slice half very thinly and add to the pan, then finely julienne the rest and set aside.

Slice the leek into 5mm rounds and add two-thirds to the pan. Slowly bring to just below boiling point – but don't let it actually come to the boil. Turn down to a simmer and cook for 8 minutes, then turn the heat off and cover with a lid. Leave to sit for 30 minutes.

Place the sea vegetables in a small bowl and pour over a cupful of water. Strain the soup into a clean pan and add the sliced fresh shiitake caps, ginger julienne, remaining leek, mirin and soy sauce.

Take the dried shiitake, which will have swollen up now, and slice them very thinly, then add these to the pan, discarding the stalks (which can sometimes be woody). Bring the soup to a simmer and cook for 3 minutes. Drain the soaked sea vegetables.

To serve, ladle the soup into 4 bowls, adding some of the sea vegetables as you go. Drizzle the sesame oil on top just as you serve it.

Kale, potato, chorizo and garlic soup

This chunky, hearty soup is very much like the Portuguese *caldo verde*. The chorizo prevents it from being a totally vegetarian soup, but adds fabulous flavour and texture. If you prefer your soup meat-free, then replace the chorizo with 2 teaspoons of *pimentón dulce* (sweet and mild Spanish smoked paprika).

serves 4–6

6 garlic cloves, peeled and quartered

4 tablespoons olive oil

4 large shallots, sliced into 5mm rings

150g cooking chorizo, diced

2 large potatoes, peeled and diced

2 bay leaves, torn in half

400g tin of chopped tomatoes with their liquid

1 litre hot water

100g kale, without too much stalk, roughly chopped

handful of chopped parsley, plus some more whole leaves for garnish (optional)

Place the garlic and olive oil in a large pot and cook over a low heat until the garlic is golden – it could take up to 15 minutes. Garlic burns easily, so keep an eye on it. Remove the garlic with a slotted spoon, reserving it.

Turn up the heat, add the shallots and sauté them until golden. Add the chorizo and cook for a further minute, stirring constantly. Add the diced potato, bay leaves and reserved garlic, and sauté, stirring occasionally, for 5 minutes.

Add the tomatoes and the litre of hot water, and bring to the boil. Stir in the kale and again bring to the boil. Add a teaspoon of salt, turn down to a simmer, cover and cook for 30 minutes.

To serve, taste and adjust the seasoning if necessary, then stir in the chopped parsley. Garnish with some whole parsley leaves if you like.

serves 6

2 white onions, sliced

4 garlic cloves, sliced

2 thumbs of ginger, peeled and thinly sliced

1 teaspoon cumin seeds

2 teaspoons mustard seeds

4½ tablespoons vegetable oil

100g chopped blanched almonds

1 ripe plantain (it must be ripe, with a brown skin), peeled and thinly sliced

400ml coconut milk

3 tablespoons tamarind paste

1 drumstick (see right), prepared as described, then gently bashed down its length and cut into 6 equal lengths

1 sweet gourd

1 tablespoon lemon juice

6 tablespoons desiccated coconut

small handful of coriander leaves

Sauté the onions, garlic, ginger and seeds in 3 tablespoons of the oil to caramelize lightly. Add the almonds and plantain, and cook for a further 2 minutes, stirring often.

Add the coconut milk, tamarind and 900ml water, and bring to the boil. Add the drumstick and simmer rapidly, covered, for 20 minutes, stirring occasionally.

Peel the gourd and cut into 4 lengthways, then remove the seedy core (a few seeds left intact are fine). Cut the pieces into chunky dice, then sauté in 1 tablespoon of the oil until softened, then add the lemon juice and take off the heat.

Fry the desiccated coconut in the remaining oil over a gentle heat until golden and remove from the heat.

Once the soup is cooked, remove the drumstick pieces and then purée the soup. It shouldn't be too fine as you want a bit of texture.

To serve, divide the soup between 6 bowls and spoon on some of the sweet gourd, coconut and coriander. Stick a drumstick piece into each bowl of soup and get your guests to gently suck on it as they eat.

Sweet gourd, almond and plantain soup

Traditionally cooked in India with lentils, drumsticks – also known as horseradish tree or moringa – resemble very stiff long, thin cucumbers. Their ridged fibrous exterior needs to be peeled off, which is best done with a small sharp knife, as you would string runner beans. Sweet gourd resembles a ridged elongated cucumber. Its cousin, the bitter gourd, or kerala, needs to be salted before cooking to remove the bitterness, but sweet gourds are subtle and mellow. You can replace the drumsticks with okra and the sweet gourd with cucumber. If you can't get plantain, then replace it with a ripe banana and a small peeled potato, which will provide both starch and sweetness. A more exotic vegetable soup I can't think of!

Curried pumpkin and swede soup with feta and caramelized red onion

If there's one thing all us New Zealanders can make it's pumpkin soup. The pumpkins we grow there are firm, thick-fleshed and full of flavour. Recently, the pumpkins available here in the UK have improved enormously – from thin-fleshed watery-flavoured ones to robust hearty beasts. If you can't find a good pumpkin, then butternut squash is a great alternative. Cooking the red onion garnish with pomegranate molasses creates an astringent sweet accompaniment that offsets the rich soup – it's very simple but works wonderfully. I'm usually no fan of ready-made curry powder, but here I'm happy to use it.

serves 4–6

1 red onion, sliced

1 white-fleshed onion, sliced

1½ tablespoons olive oil

¼ leek, sliced and well rinsed to remove any grit

3 tablespoons mirin (or 2 tablespoons caster sugar)

400g peeled and diced pumpkin flesh

400g peeled and diced swede flesh

1½ teaspoons ground turmeric

3 teaspoons curry powder (mild or spicy, it's up to you)

900ml vegetable stock (although water will suffice)

6 tablespoons double cream

125ml thick plain yoghurt

150g feta cheese, crumbled

for the caramelized red onion

1½ tablespoons olive oil

1 red onion, finely chopped

1 tablespoon pomegranate molasses (or use balsamic vinegar)

In a large saucepan, sauté the sliced red and white onions in the olive oil until they begin to caramelize, stirring often.

Add the leek and sauté for a few minutes more to soften it. Add the mirin and bring to the boil, then cook to evaporate it. Add the pumpkin, swede, turmeric, curry powder and a few pinches of salt, then cook for 2 minutes while stirring.

Add the vegetable stock or water and bring to the boil, then cover with a lid and simmer for 30 minutes, until the pumpkin and swede are cooked.

Meanwhile, make the caramelized red onion: heat the oil in a small pan and sauté the chopped red onion until caramelized, stirring often. Add the pomegranate molasses and cook to evaporate it off, then take off the heat.

Once the pumpkin is cooked, add the cream and yoghurt to the soup, and bring it to a gentle boil.

To serve, mix half the feta into the soup before ladling into soup bowls, spoon a little of the onion mixture on top and then add the remaining feta.

casseroles & curries

Butternut, peanut, pea and spinach coconut curry with cashew salad

For this recipe, I used a commercially made Thai green curry paste and also added some green bird's-eye Thai chillies. The heat was high, but the sweetness of the coconut milk and butternut squash offset it. If you prefer your curries milder, then just add less of the spicy stuff. Serve it with plain rice.

serves 4–6 as a main course

2 tablespoons vegetable oil

1 large white onion, sliced

1½ tablespoons Thai green curry paste

4 garlic cloves, roughly chopped

2 handfuls of skinless roasted peanuts, roughly chopped

1 lemon grass stalk

400ml unsweetened coconut milk

600ml hot water

2 green bird's-eye chillies, sliced

600g butternut squash, peeled and cut into large chunks

3 tablespoons Thai fish sauce (or use salt to taste)

2 large handfuls of fresh or frozen peas

250g small-leaf spinach (or use large-leaf and roughly chop it)

for the cashew salad

large handful of toasted cashews, roughly chopped

2 spring onions, sliced

handful of coriander, roughly chopped

In a large pot, heat the vegetable oil and sauté the onion until it is just beginning to caramelize. Add the curry paste and garlic, and fry for a minute, stirring often. Then add the peanuts and fry for another minute, again stirring well to prevent the mixture sticking.

Meanwhile, remove the base and the 3 hard outermost layers of the lemon grass stalk and thinly slice the remaining stalk until it gets too woody, but reserve the woody stalk.

Add the coconut milk, hot water, chillies, lemon grass slices and the reserved stalk, and bring to the boil. Add the butternut squash and the fish sauce, then simmer rapidly until the squash is almost cooked through. Add the peas and cook for a further 3 minutes, taste and adjust seasoning if necessary, then stir in the spinach and turn off the heat.

To make the cashew salad, simply mix the ingredients together.

To serve, divide the curry between bowls, scatter a little of the salad over the top and let people help themselves to more as they wish.

2 tablespoons extra-virgin olive oil

2 large red onions, sliced

1 tablespoon rosemary leaves

50g pine nuts

400g tin of chopped tomatoes, with their liquid

2 tablespoons soy sauce

1 kohlrabi, peeled, halved and cut into wedges

1 large head of cavolo nero, to yield 150g leaves (see right), roughly chopped

1 tablespoon shiro miso (white miso)

for the sweet potato miso mash

800g sweet potatoes, peeled and chopped into large chunks

125g butter

1 tablespoon roughly chopped rosemary

2 tablespoons shiro miso (white miso)

Kohlrabi, cavolo nero, pine nut and tomato stew on sweet potato miso mash

Kohlrabi must be one of the oddest-looking of vegetables – UFO and jellyfish are words I've heard used to describe it. It's lovely grated raw into salads and coleslaws, but it's most often cooked, especially in Germany and Eastern Europe. Cavolo nero – Italian for 'black cabbage' – has made inroads into our diet thanks to the growing popularity of Italian cuisine and, like Brussels sprouts, needs a good frost to enhance the flavour. To prepare it, simply pull the sword-like leaves from the thick stems. Holding the leaves in your hand, run your fingers (or a small knife) along the rib to separate the leaf from the rib. Only the leaf is edible.

Start making the sweet potato miso mash by boiling the sweet potatoes in lightly salted water until cooked.

While they are cooking, make the stew: heat a wide pan and add the oil, followed by the onions, rosemary and pine nuts. Sauté over a moderate heat, stirring frequently, to caramelize the onions, but make sure the nuts don't burn.

Add the tomatoes, soy sauce and 700ml water. Bring to the boil, cover and simmer for 10 minutes. Add the kohlrabi and cavolo nero, and mix in well. Cover and cook at a very gentle boil until the kohlrabi is just cooked, around 12–15 minutes. Mix in the miso, then taste and adjust the seasoning, if necessary.

Finish making the sweet potato miso mash, when the sweet potatoes are cooked, drain them well. Place the butter and rosemary in a small pan and cook over a moderate heat until the butter goes a light nut-brown colour. Mash the potatoes with the butter, using the miso as your seasoning. Taste it and add a little extra if needed.

To serve, divide the mash between 4 bowls and ladle the stew on top.

Grilled sweetcorn, tofu, porcini, miso and arame casserole

This casserole is a particular favourite in autumn, when the sweetcorn is still sweet and juicy and the weather a little cooler, and it is great served with steamed rice or rice noodles. As you can see, I like to serve the corn in chunks, so you'll have to use your hands to eat it. However, if you'd prefer, you could grill the corn, then shave off the kernels. Less fun, but just as tasty.

500g firm tofu (I use Japanese tofu from a Tetra Pak, which works well)

small handful of dried arame seaweed (dried hijiki would work just as well)

20g dried porcini mushrooms (or any other dried wild mushroom)

300ml boiling water

2 sweetcorn cobs, husks removed

40ml vegetable oil

1 tablespoon sesame oil

2 tablespoons shiro miso (white miso)

3 tablespoons mirin

400ml warm water

2 spring onions, sliced

Cut the tofu into 12 even-sized pieces and lay them on a triple thickness of absorbent kitchen paper. Lay 3 layers of kitchen paper on top and gently press down to draw out excess moisture, then leave to sit while you cook the corn.

Put the arame and porcini in a heatproof bowl and pour over the boiling water.

Heat a dry deepish, wide non-stick pan that has a tight-fitting lid. Brush the corn cobs with 2 teaspoons of the vegetable oil. When the pan is good and hot, add the corn. Cook over a moderate-to-high heat, with the lid on, to colour the kernels golden all over, shaking the pan often to colour them evenly. The more they're caramelized, the more flavour they'll develop – but don't let them blacken.

Once the corn is cooked, take it out of the pan and rinse the pan out with some hot water – it will splutter a bit, as it will be fairly hot, so stand back. Put the pan back on the stove and heat it up again. Add the remaining vegetable oil followed, by the sesame oil. Place the tofu in the pan and cook it until golden on both sides – this will take about 2–3 minutes on each side.

While the tofu is cooking, whisk the miso with the mirin and the 400ml warm water. Once the tofu is cooked, pour the miso mixture into the pan together with the arame, porcini and their soaking water, and bring to the boil.

Cut each corn cob into 6 pieces (it can be hard to cut through the core, so use a large knife) and add these to the pan. Cover and cook at a rapid simmer for 12 minutes. Taste and adjust the seasoning with a little soy sauce or salt, if necessary, and serve while hot, sprinkled with the sliced spring onions.

12 baby carrots, scrubbed

375ml instant couscous

375ml tepid water

1 large red onion, sliced

2 teaspoons vegetable oil

2–3 teaspoons harissa paste

1 thumb of ginger, peeled and cut into julienne strips

400g can of chopped tomatoes (or use the same weight of fresh, peeled and chopped)

2 tablespoons toasted sesame oil

400ml can of unsweetened coconut milk

1 sweet potato, peeled and cut into 5mm rounds

12 okra

for the gremolata

1 lemon

1 garlic clove, finely chopped

small handful of parsley, chopped

Okra, baby carrot, harissa and sweet potato stew

My relatives in Arkansas grow their own okra and it's a beautiful plant. It is widely cultivated throughout India and Africa, but some people here find the texture a little frightening – it can go slimy if overcooked. If you can't get your hands on harissa (a spicy North African chilli paste), then use a Thai-style red curry paste or simply a little chopped chilli. Gremolata is a traditional Italian accompaniment for osso buco (braised veal shin), but its fresh citrus flavour really complements this dish.

Cover the carrots with cold water and bring to the boil. Cook for 10 minutes, then drain.

While the carrots are cooking, place the couscous in a medium bowl and pour on the tepid water, add 1/2 teaspoon salt and mix. The couscous will swell up and be ready to eat in about 20–30 minutes, but keep stirring it every 5 minutes.

Sauté the onion in the oil until it softens, but don't allow it to colour. Add the harissa and ginger, and cook for 5 minutes, stirring often to prevent sticking. Add the tomatoes and bring to the boil, then add a teaspoon of salt, the sesame oil and coconut milk. Bring back to the boil. Mix in the sweet potato, then cover and cook at a rapid simmer until you can almost push a sharp knife through the sweet potato rounds.

Trim the stalk ends off the okra, but avoid cutting them open. Add them and the boiled carrots to the stew and cook, covered, for 4 minutes, by which time it will be ready.

To make the gremolata, zest the lemon and chop the zest finely. Mix this with the garlic and parsley. Juice the lemon and add half of the juice to the stew, then adjust the seasoning.

To serve, divide the couscous among 4 bowls and ladle over the stew. Spoon some of the gremolata over the top or serve it in a small dish for people to help themselves.

Spinach and butter bean stew on bruschetta with truffle oil

Bruschetta hails from Italy, and it's really just toast with garlic and olive oil rubbed into it. Simple as that sounds, it's a satisfying thing, much in the way that toast itself is. The stew is very simple to knock up, and if you don't have butter beans, then just use any beans you have in the cupboard — even baked beans would work! You can cook your beans from scratch, it will just take a lot longer. If you don't have truffle oil — and don't despair if you don't — then drizzle with the best extra-virgin or lemon-scented olive oil you have.

serves 4 as a lunchtime main course

2 white onions, sliced

4 garlic cloves, 3 sliced and 1 kept whole but peeled

1 bay leaf, quartered

5 tablespoons extra-virgin olive oil

2 pinches of chilli flakes (more or less to taste)

1 tablespoon roughly chopped rosemary

1 tablespoon roughly chopped sage

1 tablespoon roughly chopped oregano

400g tin of butter beans, drained and rinsed

2 tablespoons soy sauce

250g spinach (if you're using large-leaf spinach, then roughly chop the leaves)

4 large slices of good hearty bread (sourdough will give the best results)

4 teaspoons truffle oil (I prefer white truffle oil)

large handful of shaved or grated Parmesan or pecorino cheese

In a wide pan, sauté the onions, the sliced garlic and the bay leaf in 3 tablespoons of the olive oil, until they beginning to caramelize. Add the chilli flakes and herbs, and cook a further minute, stirring often. Add the butter beans, 250ml water and the soy sauce. Bring to the boil, cover and simmer for 8 minutes.

Using the back of a spoon or a potato masher, smash about a quarter of the beans — they don't need to be smooth, but just broken up a bit. Taste and adjust the seasoning with more soy sauce or salt, if necessary. Then mix in the spinach and stir until it has wilted.

Toast the bread in a toaster, under the grill or on the barbecue, and rub the slices with the whole garlic clove, then drizzle with the remaining olive oil.

To serve, place a bruschetta on each plate, divide the bean stew on top and then drizzle with the truffle oil and sprinkle with the cheese.

Parsnip, plantain, aubergine and prawn curry

By making the stock from the prawn shells, you add a delicious extra layer of flavour. If you're vegetarian, simply omit the prawns and use vegetable stock, and perhaps some shiitake mushrooms. If you can't find whole raw prawns, and you have to add ready-cooked prawns, then make the curry with a good fish or vegetable stock. Serve it with steamed rice or egg noodles. Make sure you use a ripe plantain – it will look like a large rotten banana but will taste great. If the skin isn't beginning to blacken, it won't be ripe enough; in which case, you will need to boil the peeled slices for 5–10 minutes in sweetened water until they're just beginning to soften, then drain them and add to the curry as in the recipe.

12 whole raw prawns in their shells

2½ tablespoons vegetable oil

1 thumb of ginger

4 garlic cloves, roughly chopped

1 white onion, sliced

1 tablespoon mustard seeds

½ teaspoon fennel seeds

4 green cardamom pods, squashed a little

2 star anise

pinch of saffron or ¼ teaspoon ground turmeric

1 green chilli, thinly sliced

1 large parsnip, peeled and diced

2 strips of lemon zest (just the yellow layer, not bitter white pith)

1 aubergine, stem removed and cut into large chunks

1 ripe plantain, peeled and sliced into 1cm discs

large handful of mint leaves, shredded, but not too thinly

small handful of parsley leaves, roughly chopped

Remove the heads and shells from the prawns, keeping the tail shell on if you like – I do. Heat a saucepan and add a tablespoon of the oil, then add the prawn shells, ginger and 2 of the garlic cloves, and fry over a high heat, stirring all the time until the shells turn red. Add 700ml cold water and a teaspoon of salt, and bring to the boil. Then reduce to a simmer, cover and cook for 25 minutes.

Heat a wide pan and add the remaining oil, the onion and the spices. Fry over a moderate heat until the onion colours, then add the remaining garlic, chilli, parsnip and the lemon zest, and sauté for 3 minutes, stirring often. Add 300ml water and bring to the boil, then mix in the aubergine and plantain, and strain the prawn stock over the vegetables. Bring to the boil, then cook at a rapid simmer until the parsnip is cooked (the plantain should be ready at the same time).

Taste and adjust the seasoning, if necessary. Then add the prawns to the curry and cook for around 2 minutes, when they should just be done. Mix in the mint and parsley and it's ready to serve.

frying

Deep-fried Jerusalem artichokes with aubergine yoghurt relish

This is a lovely way to eat these controversial tubers. They tend to give half the population rather bad flatulence – due to a carbohydrate they contain that we mostly can't digest. They are, in fact, a member of the sunflower family, and came originally from North America, where they were a common food among many Native Americans. The name comes from the Italian for sunflower – *girasole* – as they are not artichokes, and they're definitely not from Jerusalem.

serves 6 as a first course
600g Jerusalem artichokes
vegetable oil for deep-frying

for the aubergine yoghurt relish
1 aubergine, stem removed
2 tablespoons olive oil
1 garlic clove, chopped
½ teaspoon chilli flakes
½ teaspoon cumin seeds
100g thick plain yoghurt

Wash excess dirt off the artichokes; you may need to use a scrubbing brush or steel wool to get into their little nooks and crannies. Place in a deep pot and cover with cold water, add 1 tablespoon salt and bring to the boil, then cook until you can just insert a thin knife into them. Tip into a colander, then cut them open lengthways while they're hot (a pair of tongs and a sharp knife are required unless you have chefs' asbestos fingers). Leave them to cool down and let the steam escape from within, as this will help them cook when deep-frying.

Prepare the aubergine yoghurt relish: peel alternating lengthways strips of skin from the aubergine to leave it decoratively half-striped, then cut it into 1.5cm cubes. Mix together the olive oil, garlic, chilli and cumin. Heat a pan and add the garlic mixture, stirring to prevent it burning. Once the garlic has turned golden, add the aubergine pieces and stir for 10 seconds to coat them in the flavoured oil. Add 150ml of cold water and ½ teaspoon of salt. Cover and cook over a moderate heat for 8 minutes, stirring twice. Uncover and stir, then continue to cook uncovered, stirring frequently, until most of the liquid has evaporated. Tip on to a plate and allow to cool down. Mix in the yoghurt, then taste and adjust the seasoning, if necessary.

Heat oil for deep-frying to 180°C and deep-fry the artichokes in 2–3 batches until golden brown. Remove each batch from the oil and drain on kitchen paper, sprinkling with a little salt.

To serve, put the relish in a bowl and serve alongside the artichokes.

serves 4 as a first course

vegetable oil for deep-frying

1 small kumara, skin scrubbed but not peeled, and thinly sliced (sweet potatoes will work just as well)

1 carrot, sliced at an angle

1 courgette, sliced at an angle

16 baby asparagus tips

1 small red onion, sliced into 1cm rings

handful of flat parsley sprigs, well dried

for the ginger soy dipping sauce

1 thumb of ginger, peeled and chopped

100ml soy sauce

3 tablespoons cider vinegar or balsamic vinegar

for the beer batter

150g flour

1 teaspoon baking powder

1 tablespoon sugar

1 teaspoon fine salt

325ml beer

1 tablespoon sesame seeds

First, make the dipping sauce: mix the ginger with the soy sauce and the vinegar, and leave for at least half an hour before using.

Next make the beer batter: sieve the flour, baking powder, sugar and salt together into a bowl. Pouring slowly, whisk in all the beer, then mix in the sesame seeds. Leave to sit for 15 minutes before using.

Preheat the oven to 110°C/ gas ¼. Heat 5cm of oil in a wide pan to 180°C. Place the kumara slices in the batter and mix together then carefully drop into the oil and cook for a minute, then flip them over and cook until they're golden on the other side. Remove and drain on kitchen paper. Do the same with each of the vegetables, cooking just one type at a time, as they'll each require different cooking times. Keep the fried vegetables warm in the oven. Tip the oil through a sieve after each batch is cooked and return it to the hot pan to keep cooking, discarding the crunchy bits of batter that have dropped off.

Finally, drop the parsley into the oil and swirl it around until it stops spluttering, remove and drain.

To serve, divide the vegetables between 4 plates, garnish with the fried parsley sprigs and serve with a little bowl of the dipping sauce.

Beer-battered vegetables with ginger soy dipping sauce

Much as I like Japanese tempura vegetables, I have less success with that type of batter than I do with a good old-fashioned beer batter. So, this dish is really a Western version of the former. Any beer will do — as will Champagne. You want a yeasty fizzy liquid to help the batter work. I added a mixture of black and white sesame seeds to the batter — but nigella seeds, smoked paprika, fresh chopped herbs or even desiccated coconut will give a nice twist. You can use any vegetables, just make sure they're cut quite thinly. I also added some fried parsley, not battered, to give a fresh green garnish to the plate.

Sweet potato, red onion, smoked paprika and olive frittata

Frittata is the Italian name for what the Spaniards call a tortilla. Basically, it's a very dense omelette made with vegetables included as a core ingredient, rather than simply as a stuffing. In Spain, you're likely to get a potato and white onion tortilla, and in Italy you're more likely to get a spinach frittata.

serves 6–8 as a lunch dish with salad

1 large sweet potato (about 400g), peeled and diced

6 tablespoons olive oil

1 large red onion, sliced

½ teaspoon sweet smoked paprika (*pimentón dulce*, see page 20)

8 eggs

2 handfuls of stoned olives, roughly chopped

1 spring onion, sliced

Preheat the oven to 180°C/gas 4. Line a roasting tray with baking parchment and lay the sweet potato on it. Drizzle with 2 tablespoons of olive oil, sprinkle with salt and pepper, and roast until cooked through and lightly coloured, about 20 minutes.

While the sweet potato is cooking, heat a 24cm sauté pan (a non-stick one is great when making a frittata) and caramelize the onion in 2 tablespoons of oil, adding the smoked paprika for the last few minutes of cooking.

Break the eggs into a bowl and add the olives, spring onion and a little salt. Once the sweet potato is cooked, add it to the eggs with the onion and mix well. Place the pan over a high heat and, when it's fairly hot, add the remaining 2 tablespoons of olive oil, tilt to coat the pan base, then quickly tip in the egg mixture. Let it sit undisturbed for 30 seconds, then slowly mix it, taking the raw inner part to the outside and bringing the cooked outside into the centre. Cook it like this for 2 minutes, making sure it doesn't catch on the bottom. You can now either place the sauté pan (if it's ovenproof) in the oven and cook for 8–10 minutes, or place it under a hot grill for 6–8 minutes until it's cooked through. The frittata should be almost firm to the touch, with just a little give. Take it away from the heat and leave it to rest in the pan for 10 minutes before carefully inverting it on to a large serving plate. Leave to cool down.

A frittata is almost better after 4–5 hours than it is straight from the pan, so it's a good idea to make it ahead of time. It will keep out of the fridge in a cool place for up to a day; just make sure it's tightly covered, away from the sun and heat.

Crumbed aubergine with tomato and red pepper salsa and pea shoots

This dish makes an excellent simple summer starter, although it can be a lovely accompaniment to grilled or pan-fried fish or chicken. Aubergines have a tendency to absorb a lot of oil when they're fried – if you crumb them, they take on less, and the texture of the crunchy crumbs is a lovely contrast to the flesh inside. Pea shoots are the delicate tasty tendrils from the top of the pea plant. Known as *dau miu*, they have long been popular in Chinese cooking and in the cuisines of Southeast Asia, but they are now becoming increasingly available over here.

serves 4 as a first course

1 large aubergine, around 450–500g (or use 2 small-to-medium-sized ones)

4 tablespoons flour

2 eggs

2 large handfuls coarse breadcrumbs

few tablespoons of vegetable oil

2 handfuls of pea shoots (or use rocket, watercress or frisée)

for the red pepper salsa

1 red pepper, halved and deseeded

2 tomatoes, halved and deseeded

1 lemon

2 tablespoons extra-virgin olive oil

handful of basil leaves

2 tablespoons finely snipped chives

Chop the base and stalk end off the aubergine, then cut it into 8 even-sized discs. Add a little ground pepper to the flour and place in a medium bowl. In another bowl, whisk the eggs with a teaspoon of salt. Place the breadcrumbs in a third bowl. One by one, coat the slices with flour, shaking off excess, then dip them into the beaten egg, then into the breadcrumbs – pressing these firmly on to the slices. Once they're all coated, place on a tray in the fridge.

Make the red pepper salsa: cut the pepper and tomatoes into smallish dice. Cut both ends off the lemon and sit it upright on a chopping board. Cut the rind and pith from it. Cut the flesh into dice, discarding any pips, and mix with the tomatoes, pepper and olive oil. Season the mixture, then mix in the basil and chives.

Heat a frying pan and add a few tablespoons of vegetable oil, then cook as many aubergine slices as can fit comfortably into the pan at one time until golden all over. (If the aubergine slices are very thick, you may want to finish them in an oven preheated to 180°C/gas 4 until they're just cooked through.)

To serve, place one of the 4 largest aubergine slices on each of 4 plates. Place some pea shoots on top with half the salsa. Sit the remaining aubergine disc on top and spoon the remaining salsa and its juices on top.

1½ cups of jasmine rice (or basmati)

2 thumbs of ginger, peeled

handful of mint leaves, shredded

200ml thick plain yoghurt

2 tablespoons avocado oil (or try groundnut or a refined vegetable oil)

handful of curry leaves

4 garlic cloves, chopped

1 chilli, chopped (more or less to taste)

4 tablespoons pine nuts

2 handfuls of fresh shiitake mushrooms, stems removed and discarded (or saved for vegetable stock) and caps sliced

large handful of beans, topped (I used yellow beans)

6 tablespoons soy sauce

½ large or 1 small Chinese cabbage, shredded

small tin of water chestnuts, drained, or 12 fresh ones, peeled, cut into discs

2 teaspoons toasted sesame oil

4 spring onions, sliced into 1cm lengths

large handful of basil leaves (regular or Thai basil), torn

Rinse the rice really well in a sieve and then put it in a pot with 3 cups (750ml) of cold water. Thinly slice half the ginger and add to the rice, bring it to the boil, then put a lid on and cook on the lowest heat for 10 minutes. Turn the heat off, keep the lid on and leave for 10 minutes.

Mix the mint into the yoghurt with half a teaspoon of salt and put to one side.

When the rice is almost ready, heat the wok to a moderate heat and add the oil, curry leaves, garlic and chilli. Cook over a moderate heat for a few minutes, until the garlic begins to colour, stirring often. Add the nuts and shiitake mushrooms, and cook until the nuts begin to colour, stirring often. Add the beans and half the soy sauce, then turn the heat up and cook for a few minutes, tossing occasionally.

Turn the heat to full, then add the cabbage and water chestnuts, and begin to toss and mix until the beans are just cooked through and the cabbage is wilted. Add the remaining soy sauce and the sesame oil, together with the spring onions and basil, and cook for a further minute.

To serve, divide the rice between 4 warmed bowls and spoon the vegetables on top. Serve the minted yoghurt in a separate dish.

Chinese cabbage, bean, shiitake mushroom and water chestnut stir-fry

Stir-fries and rice are a brilliant means of making a few vegetables and leftovers go a long way – but they are also a great way to cook very fresh vegetables very quickly. Have the rice cooked before you even begin to cook the stir-fry.

The rules for the best wok frying are:

• Use a wok that's big enough – or cook the stir-fry in several batches – if the wok gets overcrowded, the vegetables will become soggy and steam rather than fry.

• Keep the heat up high once you've added the ingredients – but only ever add the oil after the wok has heated or it will burn.

• Use an oil with a high smoke point – refined oils, avocado oil, groundnut oil are all good. If using sesame oil, add it towards the end of cooking.

• If you don't have a gas hob, then use a flat-bottomed wok – a round-bottomed wok just won't heat properly on an electric hob.

Shiitake mushroom, cheese and basil fritters

These fritters make a tasty starter served with a simple tangy salad – here I used rocket, raw shiitake mushrooms and radishes, tossed with olive oil and lemon juice. They are also great as a side dish, with a vegetable stew or curry as the starch component, and make a good canapé served with a dollop of pesto on top.

serves 6–8 as a first course

70g flour

100g polenta

$^2/_3$ teaspoon fine salt

1 teaspoon baking powder

$^1/_3$ teaspoon baking soda

1 teaspoon sugar

$^1/_2$ tablespoon ground roasted coriander seeds

350g thick plain yoghurt

2 tablespoons extra-virgin olive oil

1 egg

3 garlic cloves, finely chopped or grated

2 spring onions, thinly sliced

large handful of basil leaves, coarsely shredded

12 shiitake mushrooms, stems removed and caps thinly sliced

200g firm cheese (try halloumi, feta, Cheddar or Emmental), cut into small dice

vegetable oil, for deep-frying

Sift the flour, polenta, salt, baking powder and soda, sugar and coriander seeds together.

In a large bowl, whisk together the yoghurt, 4 tablespoons of cold water, the olive oil, egg and garlic. Mix in the spring onions, basil, mushrooms and cheese, then mix in the polenta mixture. Leave to rest for 20 minutes.

Heat vegetable oil in a deep-fryer to 180°C. Scoop out a dessertspoonful of the fritter mixture and, using another dessertspoon, scrape the mixture carefully into the hot oil so that it falls off the spoon. Cook as many fritters as will comfortably fit into the fryer (they will expand a little) for 4 minutes, turning them regularly to make sure they cook evenly all over. Remove from the fryer and leave to drain on kitchen paper in a warm place while you cook the rest.

Serve as soon as all are ready, on a bed of leaves and garnished with slices of radish and shiitake mushrooms if you like.

serves 6 as a side dish

3 large starchy potatoes, peeled

1 white onion, thinly sliced

2 tablespoons poppy seeds

1 large egg (or use 1 egg plus the white of 1 extra egg)

4 tablespoons flour

1½ teaspoons baking powder

1½ teaspoons fine salt

vegetable oil for deep-frying

for the quick sweet chilli sauce

2 garlic cloves

fresh chilli to taste, chopped (I used 3 small Thai bird's-eye chillies and they were really deliciously hot)

4 tablespoons pale palm sugar, chopped or grated (or demerara sugar)

grated zest and juice of 2 limes

2 tablespoons lemon juice

1 teaspoon Thai fish sauce (or 2 pinches of salt)

First make the sauce: it is best to use a pestle and mortar, although a very small food processor will work at a pinch. Place the garlic, chopped chilli and sugar in the mortar and pound everything together. Add the lime zest and pound again. Mix in the citrus juices and fish sauce, and it's ready. Set aside.

Coarsely grate the potatoes and mix with the onion, then squeeze out excess moisture – the more you get out the better. Place in a bowl and add the poppy seeds (the eyes!), the egg, flour, baking powder and salt. Mix well and leave to rest for 10 minutes.

Heat vegetable oil to a depth of 6cm in a deep-fryer (or a pot) to 180°C. Have handy a tray lined with kitchen paper. You need to decide what size of fritters you want, then squeeze the mixture between your fingers and carefully drop it into the hot oil – but please, do be careful. You can also drop the mixture off a spoon into the oil. Cook the fritters until they're golden all over, turning them in the hot oil as they cook. As they're done, remove them from the oil and drain on the paper-lined tray.

The fritters are best eaten hot. Serve with the sauce.

Mock whitebait fritters with quick sweet chilli sauce

These fritters are the invention of my father, Bruce Gordon. They're called mock whitebait fritters because in New Zealand our whitebait (which you'll only find there and in Patagonia and parts of Tasmania) look more like elvers – tiny baby eels. When cooked they are white with black eyes – hence my adding poppy seeds to this! These fritters can be served as a party canapé if made quite small, as a starch component to a main meal, or as a late night snack – if you could be bothered setting up a deep-fryer after getting home from a party! Dad would never serve this sauce with them, but I really like it.

Spinach and cottage cheese fritters with rocket and caper salad

These fritters are excellent served as a casual first course or as a vegetable accompaniment to a main meal. They go really well with poached chicken and minted peas, or with crisp smoked bacon and a poached egg for a lazy Sunday brunch.

serves 4 as a first course or side dish

250g baby leaf spinach, washed and drained, but with a little moisture still clinging

2 eggs, beaten

5 tablespoons flour, sifted

2 tablespoons polenta, sifted

250g cottage cheese

vegetable oil or butter for frying

2 handfuls of rocket or watercress

2 tablespoons capers, rinsed

extra-virgin olive oil for drizzling

1 lemon, quartered, to serve

Heat a wide pan and add the spinach (it may be easier to cook it in several batches). Toss it around until it wilts and collapses. You'll end up with a lot less than you'd imagine – about 1½ cups. Tip it into a colander or sieve and leave to drain for a few minutes, then transfer to a bowl and let it cool.

When cool, mix in the eggs, followed by the flour and polenta, then the cottage cheese. Season well and leave to rest for 15 minutes.

Heat a frying pan and, when it's moderately hot, add a little oil or butter. Drop spoonfuls of the mixture into the pan and cook for 2 minutes, then carefully flip them over. You don't want them to colour too much; however, if they're not cooked enough before you flip them, they could fall apart, as the mixture is quite 'soft'. Once the first batch are cooked, move them to a plate while you cook the rest of the mixture.

To serve, place 2 fritters on each plate and add some rocket or watercress. Scatter with capers and drizzle with a little olive oil. Serve with a wedge of lemon to the side.

Smoked tofu and wood fungus spring rolls

Spring roll wrappers need to be at room temperature as they are then more pliable. Those I used here were 20cm square; if you can only find larger wrappers, cut them down to size, and if you can only find smaller ones you'll get quite a few more smaller rolls. Black vinegar can be bought from Chinese food stores and is absolutely delicious – not too acidic, quite sweet and with flavours of cinnamon, orange peel and star anise. If you can't find it, replace it with equal parts lemon juice, soy sauce and runny honey. Several types of dried wood fungus can be found in Chinese food stores – brown, black, purple and white – all of which will work. While not adding much flavour, they give a great texture. If you can't find smoked tofu, use firm tofu or smoked chicken.

makes 10 rolls

30g dried wood fungus, soaked for 50 minutes in 1.5 litres tepid water

200g smoked tofu, cut into batons 1cm square in section

100g beansprouts, rinsed, drained and gently patted dry

1 small can (140g drained weight) of water chestnuts, sliced (or use fresh peeled water chestnuts)

100g oyster mushrooms, pulled apart

3 spring onions, thinly sliced

large handful of basil (regular or Thai), coarsely shredded

large handful of coriander, cut into 1cm lengths (stalk and all)

ten 20cm square spring roll wrappers, at room temperature

1 egg, beaten

vegetable oil, for deep-frying

black vinegar (see left), for dipping

Drain the fungus, pat it dry and cut any tough stalks from it, then cut it into 1cm wide ribbons and put in a large bowl. Add the tofu, beansprouts, water chestnuts, mushrooms, spring onions, basil and coriander, and mix well together.

Pull the spring roll wrappers apart carefully and lay them back on top of each other. Line a tray with baking parchment. Take one wrapper at a time and lay it in front of you in a diamond shape. Brush the far corner quarter with beaten egg. Take a tenth of the mixture and lay it across the centre of the wrapper from left to right – keeping a 3cm gap clear at both ends. Take the corner nearest you and fold it over the filling, holding it quite firmly, then roll towards the middle. Fold both the left and right corners towards the centre, holding the filling quite firmly, then continue to roll away from you to give you something hopefully resembling a spring roll. If the wrapper has broken, then you're best to unroll and start again. Roll another 9 spring rolls in the same way. Lay the rolls side by side on the tray with the seam on the bottom. You can leave them for 30 minutes before cooking them, but any longer and the filling can cause the wrappers to break.

Heat oil for deep-frying to 180°C and cook the rolls in batches, bring careful not to overcrowd the fryer. Try to keep the rolls submerged as they cook and, once they are golden, remove them and transfer to a tray lined with absorbent paper. They will be incredibly hot – all the moisture from the filling having turned to steam, which will burn your mouth – so leave them for 2–3 minutes before eating, dipping them into the vinegar.

roasts, bakes & braises

Maple-roast Brussels sprouts, chestnuts and garlic

This dish is perfect with the Christmas meal, or, in fact, any celebratory gathering. These days it's fairly easy to get vacuum-packed prepared chestnuts – simple to use and with a long shelf-life, they make things a lot easier. You may want to prepare them yourselves, but one freezing winter in London I just found myself a roasted chestnut seller and bought some from him, already shelled – such men are rare now, but are well worth supporting. If you don't have maple syrup, try a mixture of dark honey and muscovado or another dark sugar – you want a little sweetness, but not too much. Just remember to keep pure maple syrup in the fridge once opened, as it will go off at room temperature.

serves 6 as a side dish

1 head of garlic, cloves separated but not peeled

400g Brussels sprouts

200g vacuum-packed chestnuts, separated

60g butter

10cm rosemary stem (or use sage, oregano or thyme)

4 tablespoons maple syrup

150ml hot water

Preheat the oven to 180°C/gas 4. Place the garlic in a large saucepan and cover with 2 litres of cold water and 2 teaspoons of salt. Bring to the boil and cook for 5 minutes.

Meanwhile, trim the Brussels sprouts of any bad leaves and trim the bases, then score a cross into each, penetrating to about 4mm.

Add the sprouts to the boiling garlic and cook for 2 minutes, then add the chestnuts, count to 20 and then drain everything.

Spread the butter over the base of a roasting dish and place the rosemary in it, then tip the vegetables on top. Drizzle with the maple syrup, season with flaky salt and lots of ground pepper and add the hot water. Seal the dish tightly with foil and bake for 40 minutes.

Take the foil off, mix it all up and continue to bake for another 10 minutes, then mix once more.

serves 6 as a side dish

100ml white wine or cider vinegar

600g salsify

10cm length of rosemary on the stem

handful of thyme

400ml double cream

8 salted anchovies, bones removed, chopped

4 tablespoons finely grated Parmesan cheese

50g softened butter

12 shelled oysters, coarsely chopped

Preheat the oven to 170°C/gas 3½. Fill a large wide saucepan with 1 litre of cold water and add the vinegar. Wash and peel the salsify as described on the right, placing them in the pan as they are done.

Add the herbs and a generous teaspoon of salt, and bring to the boil, then cook until you can just insert a sharp knife into the salsify. Drain in a colander, reserving the herbs.

Place the cream and the leaves from the reserved herb stalks in a saucepan. Bring to the boil (don't let it boil over) and simmer for 5 minutes. Add the anchovies and Parmesan, adjust for saltiness and turn the heat off.

Rub the butter over the bottom of a 1.5 litre gratin dish and then place the salsify in, trimming it to fit neatly. Spoon the chopped oysters over the salsify, grind over plenty of pepper, then pour the cream on top. Bake in the centre of the oven for 15–20 minutes, until it's golden and bubbling. Serve while piping hot.

Salsify and anchovy gratin with oysters

Salsify is occasionally called 'oyster plant', so it seemed fitting to pair it with oysters. If you're not a fishy person and want this to be oyster- and anchovy-free, then add more Parmesan and salt. Salsify usually come covered in the fine dirt in which they have been grown. You need to wash this off first, and then quickly peel them – a regular potato peeler is all you need, but, as they discolour quickly, have a pot with acidulated water ready.

Do wear gloves, as the salsify seem to coat your hands in a sticky film. Very tasty, like a crunchy potato, they are a great 'new' old vegetable to get used to again. This gratin goes really well with baked or steamed fish, as part of a vegetarian meal (without the fishy ingredients), as well as with roast lamb and chicken.

Roast fennel with olive and orange stuffing

These are delicious on their own as a main course, but equally they make a great starter (serve just one per person) or a side dish with a meat or fish main course. I like to replace the orange zest with lemon or lime for serving with grilled fish, or add lots of mint to the mixture and serve with grilled lamb chops. The roast fennel are also good to eat at room temperature, so they make a great picnic dish.

4 fennel bulbs

3½ tablespoons extra-virgin olive oil

4 tablespoons hot water

2 large handfuls of watercress (not too much stem though)

handful of mint leaves, roughly torn

1 lemon, quartered, to serve

for the stuffing

4 large handfuls of coarse fresh breadcrumbs

finely grated zest and juice of 1 large orange

2 handfuls of stoned olives, roughly chopped

2 teaspoons fresh thyme leaves (or you can also use oregano, basil, tarragon or mint)

3½ tablespoons extra-virgin olive oil

Preheat the oven to 180°C/gas 4. Trim off and discard any discoloured parts of the fennel and cut the bulbs in half lengthways. Place in a large pot, cover with cold water and add a tablespoon of salt. Bring to the boil and boil until you can insert a knife almost all the way through. Drain in a colander and leave to cool.

Meanwhile, make the stuffing by mixing together the breadcrumbs, orange zest and juice, olives, thyme, a little salt and the olive oil.

Using baking parchment, line a roasting dish just large enough to hold the fennel halves snugly. Once they are cool enough to handle, take one half at a time and hold it in the palm of your hand, cut side up. Gently pull the layers apart, being careful not to break them off, and poke the stuffing in between them. Stuff all the fennel in the same way.

Lay them in the roasting dish, stuffed side facing up, and sprinkle any remaining stuffing over, then drizzle with the oil. Add the 4 tablespoons of hot water to the dish and bake in the centre of the oven until dark golden in colour and heated through.

To serve, mix the watercress with the mint and place on 4 plates. Sit 2 stuffed fennel halves on top of each and scatter with any crumbs and juices from the roasting dish. Place a lemon wedge on the plate.

Roast shallots and rosemary

These shallots are absolutely delicious. Sweet, juicy and slightly acidic in a pleasant way, they're great served with roast meats, especially red meats, but they also go well with chunks of herb-roasted pumpkin and steamed tender-stem broccoli drizzled with pesto as a vegetarian main course. I use what are called banana shallots, because of their long shape. Round shallots will work just as well, but they take slightly less cooking, and baby red or white onions will also work, although they may take a little extra cooking. A ceramic or non-reactive metal baking dish, about 1–1.5 litres in capacity, is needed to cook these. A handy hint when baking something covered with foil in a fan oven: often the foil comes loose, so sit an upturned spoon or fork on the foil to anchor it in place.

serves 4–6 as a side dish

500g shallots

3 tablespoons extra-virgin olive oil

6 strips of lemon zest

2 bay leaves

2 tablespoons rosemary leaves

2 tablespoons cider vinegar

Preheat the oven to 180°C/gas 4. Cut a piece of baking parchment the same size as the baking dish. Cut the stem end off the shallots, but not the root end. Peel the shallots, keeping the root bit intact (this helps them stay together as they cook). Brush half the oil over the bottom of the baking dish, then place the lemon zest, bay leaves and rosemary in it and sit the shallots on top. Season generously with salt and pepper, spoon the vinegar in, together with 2 tablespoons of water, then drizzle the remaining olive oil over the shallots and place the baking parchment on top.

Seal tightly with foil (the parchment between the vegetables and the foil will prevent it sticking to the top of the vegetables) and bake for 1½ hours (around 20 minutes less for smaller shallots). Take the foil and parchment off, baste the shallots, and cook for a further 15 minutes to colour them slightly. Eat while still hot, although they reheat well.

serves 8 as a side dish

large bunch of baby beetroots with leaves attached (about 500g)

1 large red onion, sliced

4 tablespoons olive oil

2 tablespoons fresh rosemary leaves

3 tablespoons red wine vinegar or balsamic vinegar

6 garlic cloves, sliced

100ml white wine or water

a little chilli powder (optional)

50g pecorino cheese, shaved (or use Parmesan or any aged firm cheese)

Preheat the oven to 190°C/gas 5. You'll need to wash the beetroots well – they have a habit of attracting grit to the base of their leave stalks. Cut the leaves off 2cm above the top of the beets and set aside. Place the unpeeled beets in a sink of tepid water and leave to sit for 5 minutes, then carefully rub them with your fingers or a gentle brush to dislodge any dirt. Change the water and wash the leaves, then drain and keep separate.

Heat an ovenproof sauté pan that has a tight-fitting lid and sauté the onion in 2 tablespoons of olive oil until just beginning to caramelize. Add the beetroots, rosemary and a teaspoon of salt, and fry for another 2 minutes. Add the vinegar and 4 tablespoons of water, and stir it all together, then seal the pan tightly (or transfer to a roasting dish, which you'll need to seal tightly) and roast until the beets are cooked through. Beets like the ones in the photograph took 25 minutes; ones the size of walnuts will take up to 45 minutes – just poke them with a skewer, which should just go through when they're done.

Heat a wide pan and add the remaining oil, then add the garlic and sauté until golden. Add the beetroot leaves and the wine or water, and cook over a moderate heat, stirring constantly, until the leaves have wilted. Season with salt and pepper, or a little chilli powder.

Once the beetroots are cooked, toss them with the leaves and all the juices from both the pan and roasting dish. Scatter the cheese on top and serve.

Roast baby beetroot and red onions

Baby vegetables are perhaps the most faddish of all cheffy ingredients. It seems every other year they're in, the next they're out. However, of all the baby veggies, I most like beetroot and carrots, as they really do seem sweeter and are cuter to look at. The beetroot I used here were very small; but whether they're this size when you cook with them or slightly larger (up to a walnut size), the technique is exactly the same. If you buy beetroot without leaves, don't worry; just replace them with small spinach or chard leaves and cook in the same way. I like to serve these vegetables with roast meats, as you would a bowl of boiled potatoes, but they are also delicious as a starter with some fresh ricotta and chopped hard-boiled egg on top.

Roast pumpkin stuffed with wild mushrooms and hazelnuts

These little pumpkins are available only at certain times of the year, but there are many alternatives. You can make this in one large pumpkin – but it's quite expensive buying enough mushrooms to fill one, so you can bulk them out by adding a layer of sautéed regular mushrooms in the bottom. If the pumpkin is a thick-fleshed variety, it can take hours to cook, so cook the hollowed-out pumpkin with the lid askew for an hour before stuffing. These don't reheat too successfully, as it takes quite a while for the filling to get hot, so make them as you need them – although a raw stuffed baby pumpkin can be kept in the fridge for a day.

4 baby pumpkins, each about 500g

1 garlic clove, finely chopped

2 tablespoons olive oil

600g mixed wild mushrooms, cleaned thoroughly to remove twigs and the like

60g butter

1 large white onion, diced

1 leek, sliced and well rinsed if gritty

2 teaspoons mixed fresh herbs (thyme, oregano and young sage work best)

60g hazelnuts, roasted, skins removed and roughly chopped

Preheat the oven to 180°C/gas 4. If the bases of the pumpkins aren't level, carefully trim them. Cut the tops off the pumpkins, holding your knife (a narrow thin knife works best) at a 45° angle to the work surface. Scoop out the seeds with a dessertspoon and discard. Mix the garlic with the olive oil and a little salt, then brush this on the inside base of the pumpkins.

Separate the mushrooms into two groups: large and dense, and thin and delicate. Slice the larger ones into chunks.

Heat half the butter in a wide pan and, when it begins to sizzle, add the onion and cook over a moderate heat, stirring often, until caramelized to a good deep golden colour. Then add the leek and cook until that has just wilted.

Add half the mushrooms (start with the denser ones) and cook over a moderate heat until they wilt. Tip into a bowl and cook the rest in the remaining butter until they wilt. Mix together with the herbs and hazelnuts and season well.

Spoon the mixture into the hollowed-out pumpkins and place their 'lids' back on. Put into a roasting dish, adding 1cm of hot water to the dish. Bake until you can insert a skewer through the pumpkin flesh into the centre, around 70 minutes.

These are terrific served as a main course served with salad, or the slow-cooked beans on page 128.

Potato, celeriac and leek gratin with sage and feta

This is here as a guide to making gratins. Most root vegetables can be cooked like this, layered in a dish and flavoured with anything from herbs and cheeses through to spices and nuts. Then, you pour over boiling water, stock or double cream, seal tightly with foil and bake until the vegetables are cooked. The top may then be coloured under a grill. Choose a dish just large enough to hold everything, but one in which the liquids won't boil up and out of the dish. Cut out a sheet of non-stick baking parchment the same size as the dish – this will come between the vegetables and the foil, which otherwise has a habit of sticking to the top layer of vegetables. This gratin is perfect with roast salmon or chicken.

serves 4–6 as a side dish

2 tablespoons extra-virgin olive oil, plus a little extra for the baking parchment

3 large baking potatoes, cut into 5mm thick slices

100g feta cheese, crumbled

small handful of sage leaves, roughly shredded

350g celeriac (about ½ of a large one), peeled and thinly sliced

½ leek, thinly sliced and rinsed if gritty

150ml boiling water

Preheat the oven to 180°C/gas 4. Brush the 2 tablespoons of olive oil over a suitable baking dish (see left – I used one 1.5 litres in capacity) and arrange half the potato slices on the bottom of the dish. Scatter half the feta and sage on top, sprinkle with a little salt, then lay the celeriac slices on top of that, followed by the leek and the remaining feta and sage. Lay the remaining potato slices on top, pour in the 150ml boiling water, then lightly season (remembering the feta will be a little salty). Brush one side of a sheet of non-stick baking parchment the same size as the dish (see left) with a little extra olive oil and lay this side on top of the potatoes. Cover with foil and seal tightly.

Bake for 1½ hours, then remove the foil and baking parchment, and place the dish under a hot grill to colour the potatoes. Serve from the dish while piping hot.

serves 6–8

1kg large potatoes, scrubbed

2 large aubergines, stalk removed, cut lengthways into 1cm thick slices

olive oil for brushing

extra-virgin olive oil for drizzling

green leaves for garnish (optional)

for the tomato sauce

1 large red onion, sliced

1 large white onion, sliced

2 tablespoons olive oil

4 garlic cloves

2 large carrots, grated

1 large thumb of ginger, peeled and grated

½ teaspoon chilli flakes

2 bay leaves, halved

4 tablespoons sun-dried tomato paste (or use regular tomato paste)

2 large (400g) cans of chopped tomatoes

3 tablespoons coarsely chopped hard herbs (rosemary, sage, oregano, thyme)

for the cheese sauce

50g butter

3 tablespoons extra-virgin olive oil

120g flour

800ml milk, heated

2 eggs

100g feta cheese, crumbled

100g Parmesan cheese, grated

The best-ever moussaka

Some people might argue that the best moussaka should be made with minced mutton, rather than being a vegetarian dish, and that's almost correct. What I prefer, though, is to serve this veggie version with roast leg or braised shoulder of lamb and a feta cucumber salad – although it's also fabulous with a green salad as a meal in itself. The mutton version originates from the Balkans, Turkey and Greece, where plenty of sheep are to be found in the hills, but this is a great comfort-food dish, whether or not it has meat in it.

Preheat the oven to 180°C/gas 4. Make the tomato sauce: sauté both the onions over a moderate heat in the olive oil, stirring often, until just beginning to caramelize. Add the garlic, carrots, ginger, chilli and bay leaves, and cook for another 3 minutes, still stirring often. Add the tomato paste, chopped tomatoes and herbs, and bring to the boil. Cover and simmer for 20 minutes, stirring occasionally.

Meanwhile, cut the potatoes into slices about 5mm thick and simmer in plenty of salted water until just cooked, then carefully drain in a colander.

Brush the aubergine slices with oil – they absorb oil like kitchen paper does, so don't smother them – then either grill or fry until golden on both sides. They don't need to be fully cooked – a little underdone is better than fully cooked.

Make the cheese sauce: heat the butter and extra-virgin olive oil together until the butter sizzles, then add the flour and cook for 20 seconds, stirring constantly. Take off the heat and whisk in the warm milk, then return to the stove and bring to a simmer. Cook for 3 minutes, stirring constantly. Leave to cool for 5 minutes, then mix in the eggs and cheeses.

Assemble the moussaka by laying half the potatoes on the base of a 3-litre gratin dish, then spread on half of the tomato sauce, followed by half the aubergines and one-third of the cheese sauce. Repeat these layers, finishing with a layer of the cheese sauce. Drizzle with a little extra-virgin olive oil and bake for 50–60 minutes, until the top has become golden and the moussaka is heated through.

Allow to settle and cool for about 5 minutes before serving, garnished with some green leaves if you like.

Savoy cabbage, mushroom and blue cheese polenta bake

This doesn't take long to put together and makes a great hearty winter's meal. Replace the cabbage with slow-roast tomatoes, however, and drizzle pesto on the top, and it's a fantastic summer buffet dish. You can make it in advance and then reheat it; but, if you do, bake it at 160°C/gas 3 for 20 minutes before turning the heat up to colour the top. In winter, serve it with roast root vegetables and braised chard; in summer, serve it with a salad and chilled blanched beans tossed with extra-virgin olive oil and lime juice.

serves 8

1 litre vegetable stock

1 tablespoon chopped rosemary

flaky salt

250g instant polenta grains, sieved

200g blue cheese (I used Stilton, although any blue cheese will work)

100g butter

1 large white onion, sliced

½ Savoy cabbage, core removed and the leaves sliced quite thinly

2 tablespoons thyme leaves

6 tablespoons extra-virgin olive oil

300g large field mushrooms, sliced

4 garlic cloves, chopped

3 tablespoons balsamic vinegar

handful of coarse breadcrumbs

Preheat the oven to 190°C/gas 5. Using a safe pen and a dinner plate as your 'stencil', draw a circle on each of 2 sheets of baking parchment and sit each piece of parchment on an oven tray.

Bring the vegetable stock to the boil with the rosemary and 2 teaspoons of flaky salt. Slowly pour in the polenta, whisking as you go to prevent lumps forming, until it has all been added. Turn the heat down, swap the whisk for a spoon and continue to stir the polenta as it bubbles away for 3–4 minutes. It will bubble explosively, much like porridge, so be careful. Take off the heat and stir in the cheese, then spoon half in the middle of each of the baking-parchment circles. Using a wet spatula, spread the polenta out to make two identical discs. Leave to cool and firm up.

In a wide pan, heat the butter until nut-brown, then add the onion and cook over a high heat, stirring often, to caramelize it. Add the cabbage and thyme, and cover with a lid, then cook over moderate heat for 7–10 minutes, stirring every few minutes, to soften the cabbage.

Season well with salt and pepper, then tip the cabbage on to one of the polenta discs and sit the other disc on top – it may be easier to flip it on. If it breaks, it's no drama, but do try to keep it in one piece – or at least two.

Don't wash the pan out, but add 4 tablespoons of the olive oil to the pan and sauté the mushrooms and garlic until they're just cooked. Add the balsamic vinegar and cook for another minute. Tip the contents of the pan on top of the second disc of polenta, sprinkle with the breadcrumbs and the remaining oil, and bake in the top of the oven until the crumbs go golden.

Serve hot, although it can be reheated the following day.

Baked polenta with tomatoes, aubergine, peppers and mozzarella

What I love about polenta is the fact that, by the very nature of its blandness, it lends itself to so many flavours, acting like a blank canvas on which you can express yourself. In the layered polenta bake on page 78, it is enhanced with blue cheese, but here it is completely devoid of any flavour. It's the topping that makes the dish come together – a topping similar to French ratatouille or Italian caponata. Use instant polenta grains, or you'll be stirring your polenta for 40 minutes. Serve the dish with a green salad, buttered green beans and peas, or steamed broccoli and spinach.

serves 6 as a main course

250g instant polenta grains, sieved

8 tablespoons extra-virgin olive oil

2 red onions, sliced into thin rings

2 garlic cloves, chopped

2 red peppers, stems and seeds removed, cut into strips

1 aubergine, stem removed, cut into strips

6 tomatoes, cut into quarters

handful of oregano leaves

250g mozzarella, sliced

1 tablespoon thinly sliced chives

Line a shallow baking tray with baking parchment. In a large pot, bring 1 litre of water to the boil with 2 teaspoons of salt. Turn the heat to medium and whisk in the polenta. It will begin to thicken, at which point change the whisk for a spoon and cook over a moderate heat for 2 minutes, stirring constantly, but being careful that it doesn't 'plop' on to your hand. Mix in 2 tablespoons of the olive oil, then tip out on to the lined tray and form into a rough 25cm square. Leave to cool.

Once the polenta has cooled, preheat the oven to 180°C/gas 4. Heat a pot and add 3 tablespoons of the olive oil with the onions and garlic. Sauté over a moderate heat, stirring frequently, to soften the onion. Add the red peppers and aubergine, and continue to cook for another 2 minutes, stirring frequently. Mix in the tomatoes, half the oregano and 4 tablespoons of water. Cover and cook for 7 minutes, stirring twice. Season, then continue to cook until the liquid has evaporated a little.

Once the polenta has cooled, cut it into 6 even-sized pieces and place back on the lined tray. Divide the vegetable mixture between the pieces of polenta and lay the mozzarella on top. Bake in the oven until the mozzarella begins to melt and colour, about 15 minutes. While it's cooking, using a pestle and mortar, pound the remaining oregano and olive oil with 1/2 teaspoon of salt and the chives to produce a luscious green oil.

To serve, place a piece of polenta on each plate and spoon the oil over.

serves 6 as a first course or side dish

6 long Romano peppers

4–5 very ripe tomatoes, cut into thinnish wedges

bunch of basil, separated into leaves

6 stalks of thyme (or try oregano, marjoram or mint)

6 garlic cloves, thinly sliced

4 tablespoons extra-virgin olive oil

Preheat the oven to 190°C/gas 5. Lay the peppers one at a time on a chopping board and cut a T shape into them, with the long part of the T running parallel with the stalk and the top of the T at the thickest part of the pepper. Gently poke your fingers or a small knife into the pepper to remove the seeds and fibres. Poke one-sixth each of the tomato wedges, herbs and garlic slices into the pepper, trying to avoid breaking it as they will spill out if the skin breaks open. Repeat with the other peppers and remaining tomato wedges, herbs and garlic.

Place the stuffed peppers in a roasting dish and drizzle with the olive oil and plenty of salt and pepper. Bake until the skin begins to blister, but before they darken too much, about 20–25 minutes. Remove from the oven and leave to cool.

These are best eaten at room temperature, but will keep covered in the fridge for up to 2 days.

Romano peppers stuffed with tomatoes, garlic and basil

These peppers are in the Provençal style. They are lovely made in advance and then served at room temperature as part of a meal, or as a first course on their own. The peppers I used are called Romano peppers, but a regular red pepper will work, cut in half and packed with the tomatoes, garlic and herbs.

Chicory, blue cheese and sultana gratin

This dish is what might be described as *agrodolce* – sweet-and-sour. The vinegar provides the sourness – with a little help from the slightly bitter chicory – while the sugar obviously provides the sweetness. This gratin is great served with roast meats, boiled lobster or as part of a vegetarian buffet. It's best cooked in a 2-litre ceramic roasting dish, or at least in one that won't react with the vinegar.

serves 4 as a side dish

4 chicory bulbs, trimmed of any discoloured leaves and halved lengthways

2 teaspoons caster sugar

100g butter

1 large white onion, diced

100g sultanas

5 tablespoons cider vinegar or white wine vinegar

125ml double cream

100g blue cheese, crumbled (try a sharp blue cheese like Stilton or Roquefort)

Preheat the oven to 180°C/gas 4. Lay the chicory on a chopping board and sprinkle with the sugar.

Heat a wide pan and add half the butter. Once it has melted and is sizzling, add the onion and cook over a high heat until it's caramelized to a good deep golden colour, then add the sultanas and mix them in. Cook for a minute or so, stirring frequently, until the sultanas swell a little, at which point their sugars are heating up. Add the vinegar and ½ teaspoon of salt, and continue to cook until the vinegar has evaporated, stirring continuously. Tip into a roasting dish, scraping everything out.

Place the pan back on the heat and add the remaining butter. When it's sizzling, place the chicory in, cut side down, and cook over a moderate heat until they turn golden – make sure the sugar doesn't burn though. Take the pan off the heat and sit the chicory on top of the onions, cut side facing up.

Put the cream, 3 tablespoons water and the cheese in the pan and bring to the boil, then pour the mixture over the chicory. Seal the dish tightly with foil, place in the centre of the oven and bake for 35 minutes. Take the foil off and serve from the dish.

pies, tarts & quiches

Swiss chard, red pepper, mascarpone and quails' egg quiche

While shooting the photographs for this book, we had several discussions regarding the differences between a quiche, a tart and a pie. As far as I'm concerned, a pie always has a pastry top, a tart is open-topped and a quiche has a pastry bottom and an eggy, creamy filling. You can make the pastry yourself, but there are many good brands on the market from which to chose. I used both ducks' and quails' eggs in this recipe – the ducks' eggs add a pleasant richness – but I've allowed for hens' eggs to be used. If you can't get quails' eggs, then just skip them, but they do add visual appeal. Serve this warm with a green salad.

serves 8 as a light meal with salad

2 red peppers

400g shortcrust pastry

flour, for dusting

4 large banana shallots, sliced into rings

60g butter

6 garlic cloves, sliced

bunch of Swiss chard (about 450g)

500ml hot water

flaked salt

150g mascarpone cheese

4 ducks' eggs (or 5 hens' eggs)

220ml double cream

8 quails' eggs

Grill or roast the peppers to blacken the skins, turning frequently, then place in a sealed plastic bag and leave to cool. Once cool, peel off the skin, discard the stem and seeds, and cut the flesh into strips.

While the peppers are cooling, preheat the oven to 180°C/gas 4, if necessary. Roll out the pastry on a lightly floured surface and use to line a 30cm quiche dish. Line the pastry shell with baking parchment, weight with baking beans or dried pulses and blind-bake until just golden brown (12–15 minutes). Take from the oven, leaving it on, then remove the beans and lining paper.

Meanwhile, sauté the shallots in the butter to soften them, then add the garlic and cook until caramelized, stirring often to prevent sticking.

Shred the chard into 1cm pieces, keeping the leaves separate from the stalks. Once the shallots are cooked, add the stalks to them, together with the 500ml hot water. Stir it all together, then cover and boil for 8 minutes. Mix in the leaves, cover again and cook another 8 minutes at a gentle boil.

Take the lid off and season with a teaspoon of flaked salt and some pepper. Cook over moderate heat, stirring occasionally, until most of the liquid has evaporated. Add the mascarpone and half the peppers to the pan, and bring to the boil.

Meanwhile, beat the ducks' or hens' eggs and cream together, then stir into the chard mixture and pour into the quiche pastry shell. Scatter the remaining peppers on top, then crack the quails' eggs evenly over the surface.

Place the quiche on a rack in the centre of the oven and cook for 15–20 minutes. Because the egg mixture is already hot, it won't take long to cook. It's ready when the top is set and feels firm – but also has a sponginess to it. Take from the oven and leave to sit for 15 minutes before serving.

Cracking quails' eggs The best way to crack a quail's egg is to lay it on a chopping board and carefully cut the shell with a small sharp knife, not going into the egg too deeply, then pull the shell apart as you would with an ordinary egg.

Spinach, feta, mint and pine nut filo parcels

These snacks can be found throughout Turkey and Greece in one form or another. You'll find filo spirals filled with a mixture like this and sprinkled with nigella seeds on the streets of Istanbul, and similar triangles in the Greek shops in Melbourne. They are great eaten on the run, as part of a picnic, or as a first course with a green salad. You can make the mixture up to 2 days in advance.

makes 8 parcels

500g small-leaf spinach (don't bother removing the stalks if the leaves aren't too large)

12 mint leaves, shredded

150g butter

100g pine nuts

3 tablespoons toasted sesame seeds (I used a mixture of black and white)

200g feta cheese, roughly broken into small cubes

16 sheets of filo pastry, about 30x12cm

Preheat the oven to 180°C/gas 4. Wash the spinach thoroughly, then drain it well in a colander. Heat a wide pan and cook it over a high heat – the moisture still clinging to the leaves should be enough to steam it. The spinach will be easier to cook in 3–4 batches, tossing it with tongs to wilt it. As each batch is cooked, tip it into the colander to drain. Once all of the spinach is cooked, lay it on a flat tray to cool. When it is cool enough to handle, squeeze out excess water and place in a bowl with the mint.

Heat the butter in a small frying pan and cook until it just begins to go a nut-brown colour. Tip the butter into a bowl, then put the pan back on the heat – ideally with a little of the butter still in it. Add the pine nuts and cook over a moderate heat until they become golden, stirring or shaking the pan to prevent them burning. Add two-thirds of the sesame seeds to the pan and lightly toast them, then tip the seeds and nuts over the spinach. Add the feta and a little salt and pepper and mix together.

Keeping the filo in one pile, take off one sheet, lay it on a work surface so that one of the short sides faces towards you and brush the sheet generously with some of the melted butter. Lay another sheet on top and brush that with butter. Take one-eighth of the filling, a piece about the size of a golf ball, and place it just in from the bottom left-hand corner. Taking the bottom right-hand corner, fold it diagonally over to the left side. Now take the pointed end facing you, and fold it away from you, keeping the left-hand side of the pastry even and straight. Using the longest side of the triangular 'package' you have made, fold it diagonally so that the bottom left-hand corner moves to the right-hand side. Now lift the bottom right-hand corner away from you, sealing the filling inside the many layers of filo. Tidy up any pastry overhangs, brush with butter and flip the triangle over, sealing the pastry seams. Do the same with the remaining filling and sheets of pastry. Brush with the remaining butter – if you run out melt some more.

Sprinkle with the remaining sesame seeds and bake until golden, about 20–25 minutes. Take from the oven and serve warm, or leave to cool and eat within 48 hours if kept in the fridge. They can also be reheated to crisp them up a little.

serves 4 as a light meal with salad

flour, for dusting

300g puff pastry

1 egg yolk, beaten

1 tablespoon sesame seeds (I used a mixture of white and black; poppy seeds are also good)

2 sweet potatoes, scrubbed

1/2 small pineapple, peeled and cored

2 tablespoons extra-virgin olive oil

200g green beans, trimmed

for the tahini, chilli and lemon grass dressing

10cm piece of lemon grass stalk, base and outer 2 layers discarded, thinly sliced

1/2 red chilli, sliced (more or less to taste)

1 garlic clove, peeled

small handful of coriander leaves

3 tablespoons tahini

4 tablespoons lemon juice

3 tablespoons extra-virgin olive oil

On a lightly floured surface, roll the pastry out into a 15x24cm rectangle and allow to rest in the fridge for about 30 minutes.

Preheat the oven to 220°C/gas 7 and line 2 baking trays with parchment. Take the pastry from the fridge and cut it into 4 equal-sized rectangles, measuring 15x6cm. Put them on one of the prepared baking trays, brush with the beaten egg yolk and sprinkle with the sesame seeds.

Bake in the middle of the oven until they are golden and well risen, around 15–18 minutes, then turn the oven down to 200°C/gas 6 and keep them cooking for another 8 minutes or so, while you prepare the rest of the dish.

Cut the sweet potato and pineapple into slices 1cm thick and lay on the other baking tray. Brush with 1 tablespoon of the olive oil, season and place in the top of the oven.

Once you've put the tray of potato and pineapple in the oven, take the pastry out, split it in half horizontally and separate the tops and bottoms. Return them to the oven to dry them out for 5 minutes, then remove and place on a cake rack.

Once the sweet potato is cooked (insert a knife into it to test), remove the tray from the oven.

Heat a heavy-based pan, ideally non-stick, and fry the pineapple in the other tablespoon of oil to colour it on both sides, then place back on the baking tray.

While all of this is cooking in the oven, make the dressing. This is best done with a pestle and mortar, or you can chop everything very finely. Pound the lemon grass, chilli, garlic and 1/2 teaspoon of salt to a coarse paste. Pound in the coriander, then mix in the tahini, lemon juice and olive oil.

Blanch the beans and keep them hot.

To serve, place a pastry bottom on each of 4 plates, then pile the sweet potato and pineapple on top. Add the beans, then drizzle with the dressing and lastly put a pastry lid in place. Eat while still warm

Roast sweet potato, pineapple and bean pastries with tahini, chilli and lemon grass dressing

I like having sheets of rolled puff pastry in the freezer. Here I bake rectangles of it to use to sandwich vegetables and a tasty dressing. While not exactly a millefeuille ('thousand leaves'), it's near enough, give or take 990-odd layers! The dressing may separate if it sits too long, but keep it out of the fridge and stir briskly just before serving. Kumara works as well as the sweet potato, as does sliced pumpkin or squash, and runner beans or asparagus instead of beans. The pineapple may seem odd – but trust me, it works well. Serve the pastries with a simple leaf salad.

Butternut, pecan, ricotta and sage pasties

These pasties require no baking tins, so can be knocked up quite quickly – even quicker if you buy pre-rolled sheets. You can make them any size you want. For a starter, they can be made with discs of pastry the size of a saucer; for a big group, roll out a large square, then fill and fold in half to give you a rectangle that you can simply slice across. Pumpkin and kumara also work really well in these pasties, and you can replace the pecans with walnuts, hazelnuts or pine nuts. If you don't have pumpkin seed oil, you could add walnut or argan oil, or a flavoured olive oil instead. Serve the pasties with a leaf salad, a bean and pea salad dressed with mint and lemon infused oil, or some grated raw beetroot tossed with lemon juice and olive oil.

makes 6

1kg butternut squash, peeled, seeds removed and cut into 1.5cm cubes

1 red onion, thinly sliced

2 tablespoons extra-virgin olive oil

20 sage leaves, shredded

800g puff pastry

120g toasted pecans

500g ricotta

4 tablespoons pumpkin seed oil

1 egg

3 tablespoons flour

Preheat the oven to 200°C/gas 6 and line a baking tray with parchment. Mix the butternut squash, onion, olive oil and half the sage together, season with salt and a little pepper and lay on the lined baking tray. Roast until the squash is cooked (a knife goes through it easily), then take from the oven and leave to cool.

Divide the pastry in half and roll each half out to a 60x20cm rectangle. Using a 20cm diameter plate, cut out 3 rounds from each piece. Lay these on a tray and put in the fridge to rest for at least 20 minutes.

Once the butternut squash has cooled, tip it into a large bowl and mix in the pecans, ricotta and pumpkin seed oil, making sure you don't crush the butternut.

Take the pastry rounds from the fridge and allow them to come to room temperature.

Beat the egg with a pinch of salt and brush the pastry completely on one side with the egg-wash – it'll be easier to do this one piece at a time. Take one-sixth of the butternut squash mixture and dollop it in the centre of a pastry round, then carefully fold the pastry in half, making sure the filling doesn't ooze out. Dip a fork in the flour and use it to press down and seal the edges. Try to squeeze out any excess air as you do this – otherwise it can make the pastie pop open in the heat of the oven. As you finish each pasty, place it on a tray lined with parchment. Brush the remaining egg wash over the pasties and prick each one several times with the fork.

Bake for 25–35 minutes, until the pastry is golden and cooked through. Eat them straight from the oven or leave them to cool and take on a picnic.

serves 4 as a light meal with salad

300g shortcrust pastry

flour, for dusting

60g diced bacon (or pancetta or chorizo)

½ teaspoon sweet pimentón

50g butter

1 large potato, cut into 1cm dice

250ml single cream

120ml hot water

1 large handful of raw spinach, washed and coarsely shredded

2 eggs, plus 1 yolk, lightly beaten

8 large black olives, stoned and halved

Roll out the pastry on a lightly floured surface and use to line a 24cm round or 20cm square quiche dish. Allow to rest in the fridge for 30 minutes.

Preheat the oven to 180°C/gas 4. Line the pastry shell with baking parchment, weight with baking beans or dried pulses and blind-bake until just golden brown (12–15 minutes). Take from the oven, leaving it on, then remove the beans and lining paper.

In a wide pan, sauté the bacon and pimentón in the butter until beginning to crisp up, stirring often. Add the potato and cook for a further 2 minutes, stirring often. Add the cream and the 120ml hot water, and bring to the boil. Then gently boil until the potato is almost cooked, around 5–8 minutes. To test, cut a piece with a sharp knife – it should offer a little resistance.

Keeping the pan on the heat, stir in the spinach until it wilts. Take off the heat and then quickly mix in the egg and a little seasoning – the bacon will already be salty, so go easy with this. Pour the mixture into the pastry case and dot the olives over the top, poking them into the mixture slightly.

Place the quiche dish in the centre of the oven and bake until the egg has set, around 15–20 minutes. Take from the oven and leave to cool for 10 minutes before serving – although this is equally delicious eaten cold.

Spinach, potato, bacon and olive quiche

This reminds me of the bacon and egg pies I often ate as a child growing up in New Zealand. If you don't want bacon in your quiche, however, then you can replace it with sliced leftover roast chicken or duck, smoked salmon, mackerel or eel, adding them to the mixture with the eggs. If you want to make your quiche vegetarian, then increase the *pimentón* (Spanish smoked paprika) to 1 heaped teaspoon – the flavour is wonderful and your guests will assume you have used some smoked meat. Any type of potato will work with this, even kumara or sweet potato, just make sure you don't overcook them. Serve the quiche with a tomato and basil salad.

Celeriac, leek, black bean and ginger lattice pie

I have to say that, in cooking all the recipes in this book, I have come to enjoy the flavour of celeriac even more than I did when I began – it's a great vegetable and one I hope we all see more of. Here I've teamed this most European of vegetables with Chinese star anise and black beans, and it's gone deliciously well. The lattice effect looks very impressive and it's so simple to do – read on! Serve with wok-fried Oriental greens or sautéed spinach.

serves 6–8 as a light meal

flour, for dusting

500g puff pastry

1 egg, beaten

1 celeriac (around 500g), peeled and cut into coarse 2cm dice

3 tablespoons olive oil

2 leeks, sliced and rinsed if gritty

50g ginger, cut into julienne strips

2 teaspoons ground star anise

300ml double cream (or use unsweetened coconut milk)

4 tablespoons Chinese salted black beans, rinsed and drained

3 tablespoons grated Parmesan cheese

Preheat the oven to 200°C/gas 6 and line a baking tray with parchment. On a lightly floured surface, roll the pastry out and use to line a 25cm fluted loose-bottomed tart tin, then brush it all over with the egg and place in the fridge to rest while you do the rest of the preparation.

Gather all the pastry trimmings together then roll out into a rectangle 26cm long and 5mm thick and place on a tray in the fridge.

Lay the celeriac on the lined baking tray and drizzle with half the oil. Season well and roast until cooked, around 20 minutes, tossing a few times. It's cooked when you can just insert a knife through it – celeriac has a lovely firm texture, so it will never go completely soft when roasted.

While the celeriac is roasting, sauté the leeks and ginger in the remaining oil in a large sauté pan until softened and beginning to colour. Add the star anise and sauté for another minute, stirring all the time. Then add the cream and black beans, and bring to the boil. Simmer until the cream has reduced by half, then turn the heat off.

Take the tart tin from the fridge and spoon the leek mixture into it. Press the celeriac gently into the leek mixture, as you would a mosaic, then sprinkle with the Parmesan.

Take the rectangle of pastry from the fridge and cut it into thin long strips. Brush the rim of the tart shell with egg, then lay strips of the pastry across the tart from left to right, pressing them firmly into the rim. Turn the tart 90° and lay more strips across the tart to give you a lattice effect.

Brush each strip with egg, then place on a baking tray in the centre of the oven and bake for 30 minutes, until the pastry has gone golden and is cooked. Serve warm.

noodles, rice & grains

Artichoke, watercress, olive and halloumi pasta with preserved lemon

This recipe is one of those magic dishes you can make from store cupboard items, provided you've done a little wise deli shopping. Choose a good brand of artichokes, preferably in olive oil, and interestingly shaped pasta. You could have this knocked up in under 15 minutes as long as you can manage three pots or pans on the stove at once.

350–400g dried pasta (depending on how hungry you are)

vegetable oil for deep-frying

200g halloumi, cut into 1cm dice

2 tablespoons olive or avocado oil

large handful of stoned olives

½ green chilli (more or less to taste)

250g jar of artichoke wedges in olive oil, drained but reserving the oil

large bunch of watercress, cut into 2cm lengths, stems and all (rocket also works well)

2 tablespoons diced preserved lemon (see below)

Bring a large pot of lightly salted water to the boil and cook the pasta until al dente or according to the instructions on the packet (usually around 6–8 minutes in boiling water), then drain (don't refresh), reserving half a cup of the water.

Meanwhile, heat about 600ml vegetable oil to 180°C in a small pan. Carefully add the halloumi all at once and cook it until it becomes golden. Remove with a slotted spoon and drain on absorbent paper.

While the pasta and halloumi are cooking, heat a wide deep frying pan and add the olive or avocado oil, the olives and chilli. Fry over a moderate heat so that the olives and chilli sizzle. Add the artichokes and warm them through.

Add the still-hot drained pasta to the pan together with the reserved cooking water, the halloumi and watercress and half the preserved lemon. Toss together with salt and freshly ground pepper and divide among 4 warmed bowls. Drizzle on some of the artichoke oil and scatter on the remaining preserved lemon. You can serve this with grated Parmesan, but it's not necessary.

Preserved lemon This is a delicious North African condiment, made by preserving lemons in salt for a few months. It is widely used there for flavouring things like soups and is generously dolloped on tagines. The rind is eaten and the fleshy inside mostly discarded. If you can't find preserved lemons, you can make a relatively quick substitute. Cut a lemon lengthways into quarters. Slice the flesh away from the rind with a sharp knife and squeeze the juice out between your fingers. Place the skin in a pot and cover with 600ml cold water. Bring to the boil and drain. Repeat this process 3 times altogether. After the third draining, add the lemon juice to the skins with just enough water to cover them and simmer for 10 minutes with a lid on. Leave to cool and they are ready to use.

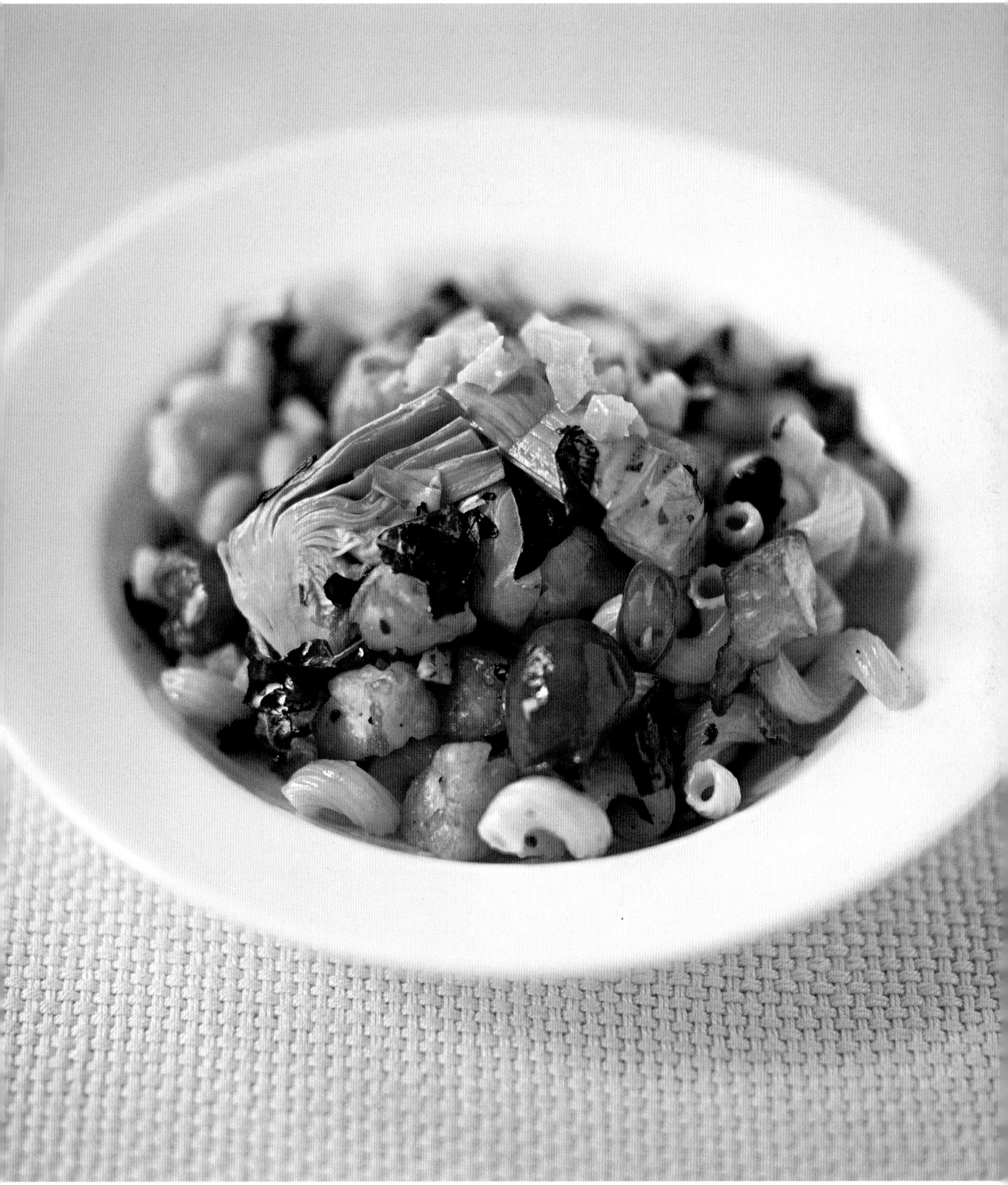

Linguine tossed with courgettes, pumpkin seeds and green beans

Pasta is one of the world's great comfort foods and, like polenta and potatoes, it is the blandness that is the basis of the appeal. The flavours you add to it, whether a meat- or vegetable-based mixture or sauce, are what makes the dish. But not quite. There is pasta and then there's pasta. Next time you shop for some, buy one of the more artisan types. They'll generally have a more interesting texture and flavour, and this only enhances the finished dish. You can omit the chilli if you prefer, but I'd rather you just added less than leave it out completely – it brings all the flavours together. The pumpkin seeds, pepitas, can be cooked up to a week in advance.

2 handfuls of pumpkin seeds

4 tablespoons extra-virgin olive oil

flaky salt

400g dried linguine

1 red or green chilli, thinly sliced into rings

4 banana shallots, thinly sliced

1 large garlic clove, chopped

200g fine green beans, topped

8 tablespoons hot water

1 large courgette, cut into Asian julienne (see below)

large handful of finely grated Parmesan or pecorino cheese

Preheat the oven to 160°C/gas 3 and line a baking tray with baking parchment. Mix the seeds with 1 tablespoon of the oil and a few pinches of flaky salt, and bake on the lined tray until they colour slightly, about 10–15 minutes, stirring them once or twice to ensure even cooking.

Bring a large pot containing 2–3 litres of lightly salted water to the boil and add the linguine, then cook until it's done to your liking. I cook mine so that it has the slightest bite to it, which will take anywhere from 7 to 10 minutes, depending on the brand of pasta. Tip it into a colander and sit an inverted plate on top to keep it warm.

Return the pot to the heat and add the remaining oil, the chilli, shallots and garlic. Sauté until the shallots have wilted and are beginning to colour, then add the beans and toss them in the mixture. Add 6 tablespoons of hot water, cover and cook for 2 minutes. Add the courgette to the pot with another 2 tablespoons of hot water, stir and sit the pasta on top. Cover again and cook for another minute.

Tip into a bowl, toss together with half the cheese and divide between 4 serving bowls. Serve the remaining cheese in a small dish.

To cut vegetables into Asian julienne
Cut them lengthways at an angle into slices about 3mm thick. Lay the slices on top of one another and cut these lengthways into strips, again about 3mm thick (see far right).

serves 6 as a main course

500g cavolo nero, prepared as described on page 31

800g sweet potato, peeled and cut lengthways into 5mm thick slices

800g red onions, thinly sliced

8 garlic cloves, sliced

200ml boiling water

2 heaped tablespoons chopped hard herbs (use individually or a mixture of thyme, sage, rosemary or oregano)

170g uncooked sheets of lasagne

for the cheese sauce

900ml milk

120ml olive oil

80g flour

2 bay leaves, both cut into 3

150g coarsely grated Gruyère cheese

Preheat the oven to 170°C/gas 3½ . Bring a large pot of lightly salted water to the boil and cook the cavolo nero for 4 minutes, then remove it from the water and drain in a colander. Add the sweet potato to the water in the pot and cook it for around 5 minutes, to the stage where you can just insert a knife through the flesh. Remove the cavolo nero from the colander and carefully tip the sweet potatoes in. Squeeze out as much excess moisture from the cavolo nero as you can, then roughly chop it.

Make the cheese sauce: bring the milk almost to the boil in a pan. In another pan, around 1.5 litres in capacity, add 5 tablespoons of oil, the flour and bay leaves, and cook over a moderate heat, stirring constantly, until the flour is sizzling. Take the pan off the stove and whisk in the hot milk, then return the pan to the heat and bring to a simmer. Cook for 2 minutes, stirring constantly as the sauce thickens. Take off the heat and stir in two-thirds of the cheese and season. Divide the sauce into two and mix the chopped cavolo nero into one half.

In a wide pan, sauté the onions and garlic in the remaining oil until they caramelize. Add the boiling water and let it bubble, then mix in the herbs and season.

Tip half of the onion mixture into the baking dish (see right) and level it out. Place half the pasta sheets on top, breaking them to fit in nicely. Next, add a layer of the plain cheese sauce, followed by a layer of the sweet potatoes. Add another layer of the pasta, followed by the cavolo nero cheese sauce, then the rest of the onions. Bake in the centre of the oven for 50 minutes, then spread the remaining cheese on top and grill until the cheese is golden and bubbly.

Sweet potato, cavolo nero and Gruyère lasagne

This isn't the sort of dish you'll want to knock up on the spur of the moment, as there are quite a few steps involved, but you can make it the day before and then gently reheat it in time for lunch or dinner. Cavolo nero is a lovely Italian green veg, although its name translates as 'black cabbage'. I like to use Gruyère or Jarlsberg in lasagne, as they give an unexpected twist to the flavour, although any good firm tasty cheese, or even a sharp goats' cheese, will be delicious. Serve this with a simple salad or steamed greens. Use a baking dish that's at least 6cm deep and with about 3 litres capacity.

Aubergine, black bean, spinach and ginger rice noodles with roast cod and tomatoes

Like all stir-fries, this dish relies on being totally prepared before you begin cooking. You'll need all the ingredients chopped, soaked and ready to go. It's important to have the fish cooking before you heat your wok, as once the noodles and vegetables are cooked, you'll want to serve them straight away. Here I use cod – but you can use whatever fish you fancy. Tamari is a high-quality Japanese wheat-free soy sauce, so, combined with the rice noodles, this dish is a welcome treat to people with a wheat allergy. A large wok is needed to make this easily; if you only have a small one, cook things in two batches.

200g dried rice noodles

4 thickish pieces of cod fillet, each about 170g, scales and bones removed

4 plum tomatoes

3 tablespoons Chinese salted black beans, rinsed and drained

1 tablespoon grated palm sugar (or use demerara)

4 tablespoons tamari

2 tablespoons lime juice

1 tablespoon toasted sesame oil

2 aubergines

1 carrot, peeled

5 tablespoons vegetable oil (groundnut and avocado oils work well in the wok)

4 garlic cloves, sliced

2 fingers of ginger, peeled and julienned

1 red chilli, sliced (more or less to taste, but keep the seeds in)

2 large handfuls of spinach

Soak the noodles in plenty of very warm water for at least 20 minutes. Season the cod on both sides and leave to come to room temperature.

Cut the tomatoes in half lengthways, then cut each half into 3 wedges. Using a thin sharp knife, cut the seeds from them and chop these seedy bits roughly and put in a bowl. Place the tomato pieces in another bowl.

To the bowl with the tomato seeds, add the black beans, sugar, tamari, lime juice and sesame oil, and mix together.

Remove the stalks from the aubergines, then cut at an angle of 45° into 5mm slices. Lay these on top of each other and cut into julienne, then put in a bowl. Cut the carrot the same way and place in another bowl.

Take a heavy-based pan (ideally non-stick) which has a tight-fitting lid and heat it with the lid off. Add a tablespoon of the vegetable oil and place the cod in it, skin side down. Cook for 2 minutes on a medium-high heat. Scatter the tomato pieces over and around the cod, and put the lid on. Turn the heat down and cook until the fish is medium-rare (after about 5 minutes, prise the flesh apart a little - it should be translucent in the middle). Take the lid off the pan and remove from the heat.

At the point when you've got the tomatoes in and the lid on the fish pan, also place the wok on the heat and add a tablespoon of oil together with the garlic, ginger and chilli, and cook over a moderately high heat, stirring constantly, until they begin to colour. Tip them and the oil into a small bowl and put the wok back on the heat.

Add another tablespoon of the oil and cook the carrot until it begins to colour and soften, then tip back into its bowl. Add 2 tablespoons of oil to the hot wok and cook the aubergine julienne for about 5 minutes, tossing frequently, until it too begins to colour and soften.

Drain the rice noodles in a colander or sieve and add these to the wok with 3 tablespoons water, the carrots and spinach, and toss it all together.

After half a minute, add the tomato bean mix and cook until the spinach wilts and the noodles are warmed through, tossing continuously over a high heat.

To serve, divide the noodles between 4 bowls, sit a piece of cod on each, spoon the tomatoes around that and scatter the fried ginger mix on top.

serves 4–6 as a main course

100g butter

2 teaspoons fennel seeds

400g butternut squash, peeled, deseeded and diced

1 leek, thinly sliced and rinsed if gritty

2 red onions, thinly sliced

2 bay leaves, halved lengthways

6 garlic cloves, chopped

300g barley

flaky salt

1.75–2 litres simmering vegetable stock

150g grated Parmesan cheese

Heat a wide pan and add the butter and fennel seeds, then sauté for a minute, stirring often. Add the butternut squash with 1/2 teaspoon of coarsely ground black pepper and sauté for 2 minutes over a moderate heat, stirring often.

Remove the butternut squash from the pan with a slotted spoon (don't worry if any fennel seeds remain), then add the leek, onions, bay leaves and garlic, and sauté until the onions are just beginning to caramelize. Add the barley to the pan and stir for a minute, then return the butternut squash to the pan, together with 1 teaspoon of flaky salt. Mix everything together, then pour in 1 litre of the stock. Stir well while it comes to the boil, then turn the heat down to a simmer, cover and cook for 10 minutes. Now you just continue to cook it like an ordinary risotto, stirring in about half a cup of simmering stock every 3–4 minutes until it's all absorbed and the barley is just tender.

Stir in the Parmesan, taste and adjust the seasoning, if necessary, and serve immediately.

Butternut, barley and Parmesan risotto

I'm the first to admit that a risotto should really be made with rice, but this is cooked in exactly the same way (in fact, you could use risotto rice), but with barley – a grain that is very, very good for you. The texture of this dish differs from a rice risotto because the barley grains remain quite plump and give a lovely texture to the finished dish. It reheats well, too, so if you have any left, just pop it in the microwave the following day. It is lovely as either a starter or a main course if served with steamed greens.

Cauliflower couscous

In Spain in 2003, I ate at one of the world's most famous restaurants — Ferran Adria's El Bulli. The food was quite bizarre, all 32 courses of it. However, I had heard that he once served cauliflower couscous, which I found an intriguing concept, so I had to play around with it. No doubt, his method involves pipettes and alginates, but this is how we make it at The Providores. It's delicious served with grilled pork chops, garlic roast pumpkin or sweet potatoes, or pan-fried mackerel.

serves 4–6 as a side dish
180g instant couscous
250ml tepid water

300g cauliflower (just use the florets and the smaller stems, not the thick main core)
2 tablespoons extra-virgin olive oil

In a medium-sized bowl, mix the couscous with the tepid water and 1 teaspoon of salt, and leave it to absorb the water.

Bring a pot of lightly salted water to the boil and add the cauliflower, making sure it is completely submerged, then boil for 4–5 minutes until it's almost cooked – don't overcook it. (Or, you can steam it.) Drain in a colander and put into a bowl of iced water for 2 minutes.

Drain it again, then place in a food processor and blitz in several short bursts, scraping down the side of the bowl each time, to produce coarse crumbs, as it were.

Mix these 'crumbs' into the couscous together with the olive oil and a generous amount of freshly ground black pepper. It will keep, covered, in the fridge for a day; just mix it together well before serving to loosen it up.

serves 6–8 as a light meal

2kg selection of trimmed raw or blanched fresh vegetables, as on the right

3–4 hard-boiled eggs, shelled and halved

prawn crackers (see below)

coriander sprigs

for the saffron rice

1 cup of white rice (although not traditional, try using basmati)

2 good pinches of saffron

1/4 teaspoon salt

for the quick peanut sauce

200ml unsweetened coconut milk

5 tablespoons chunky peanut butter

2 tablespoons soy sauce

First prepare the saffron rice: rinse the rice really well in a sieve and then put in a pan with 2 cups of cold water. Add the saffron and salt and bring to the boil, then cover and cook on the lowest heat for 10 minutes. Turn the heat off and leave, still covered, for 10 minutes more.

Make the quick peanut sauce: whisk everything together to combine, adding extra coconut milk if too thick – it should be spoonable.

Serve the vegetables nicely arranged on plates alongside a pile of the rice. Garnish with the halved eggs, prawn crackers and sprigs of coriander. You can either serve the sauce in little individual pots as here, or spoon it over the top of the vegetables.

Prawn crackers these come in many forms; the best are from Thailand, Malaysia or Indonesia – I find the Chinese ones, multicoloured and fluffy, are the least appealing. You can find them already deep-fried, but if you buy the uncooked ones, all you need to do is heat 3cm of vegetable oil to 180°C in a pan and fry them just a few at a time until they puff up, flipping them over a few times, then drain on absorbent paper.

Balinese gado gado with saffron rice

When I first flew to Indonesia in 1985, it was to Bali that I headed. They have the most delicious food, but it's gado gado I will always associate with the island. I ate it every day and it ranged from the most delicious salad to the most awful stewed cabbage. In its delicious format, it is made up of cold crisp vegetables, chunks of tofu (both fresh and deep-fried), grilled tempeh (another soya bean product), hard-boiled eggs and peanut sauce, and occasionally with toasted fresh coconut. It's a lovely summer dish – and the only recipes you'll need here are the rice and the simplest peanut sauce ever. Otherwise, all you have to do is select really fresh vegetables and then decide whether to serve them raw or blanched, although a mix of both works best.

Spaghetti squash and quinoa salad

As I mentioned in my recent book *Salads*, quinoa is an ancient Inca grain — very nutritious, with a lovely nutty taste and texture. Spaghetti squashes are interesting vegetables because they have a really unusual texture when cooked and they lack a pronounced flavour. This salad is also lovely served as a canapé, wrapped up in grilled thin slices of aubergine, like little sausage rolls, or alongside a fish or white meat dish. If you can't get the squash, then cut butternut squash or pumpkin into small dice and steam or roast them, or try it made with finely julienned kohlrabi or jícama (yam bean).

serves 6–8 as a first course

½ spaghetti squash, around 600–700g (keep the seeds intact as it holds together better while cooking)

flaky salt

100g quinoa

handful of parsley leaves

handful of mint leaves, shredded

3 tablespoons lemon or lime juice

4 tablespoons extra-virgin olive oil

Place the squash in a pot large enough to hold it comfortably (it may be easier if you cut it across in half). Cover with cold water and bring to the boil, then add 2 tablespoons of flaky salt and cook until it's done. It's ready when you can just insert a knife through the skin into the seed cavity. Remove from the pot and place in a colander, cavity side facing down, to drain.

Tip the quinoa into a fine sieve and rinse really well under warm running water for 30 seconds (the grain has a bitter natural coating). Bring 1 litre of water to the boil, add the quinoa and cook until done. The grains will begin to unfurl a little. They'll remain crunchy, but you don't want them underdone; it will take between 10 and 18 minutes. Drain them in a fine sieve and leave to cool.

With a spoon, scoop the seeds and their fibres from the squash and discard, then, using the same spoon, scrape the flesh out, running the spoon just beneath the surface to get the fibres out. Remove all of the fleshy fibres and place in a large bowl.

To serve, simply add the quinoa and the remaining ingredients to the squash and gently, but thoroughly, toss it all together, seasoning to taste.

Swiss chard, Parmesan and mascarpone risotto

Risotto isn't hard to make. All you need to remember is that the stock should be hot when you add it. The rice has ultimately to have a lovely texture (although Italians have hugely differing ideas about whether rice should be served soft or al dente — so you can't really go wrong) and you can never cook too much! It reheats well the next day, but is even better turned into fritters — roll it into balls, roll these in polenta or breadcrumbs and fry. The Italians would never eat risotto as a main course, but in winter I think it's a great idea when served with steamed greens and crusty bread. I always use volume measurements when making risotto; so you'll need a measuring jug for the rice.

serves 4–6 as a main course

2 litres vegetable stock (you'll need almost all of this but you may have some left over)

600ml risotto rice

3 tablespoons olive oil

50g butter

1 large leek, sliced (use both the green and white part of the leeks, and wash it if it looks gritty)

2 bay leaves, cut in half

2 teaspoons flaky sea salt

500g Swiss chard

3 tablespoons fresh thyme leaves

200g mascarpone

2 tablespoons fresh oregano leaves

3 good handfuls of grated Parmesan cheese

4 tablespoons extra-virgin olive oil

You'll need a pot with a capacity of 4–5 litres. Keep the stock simmering in another pan on the back of the stove. Heat the pot and add the rice and olive oil and cook over a moderate-to-high heat to colour and toast the rice lightly. This may seem a little odd, but the toasting adds another layer of flavour to the finished dish.

Once the rice is toasted, tip it into a heatproof bowl and place the pot back on the stove. Add the butter and let it cook to a nut-brown colour, then add the leek and bay leaves, and sauté until wilted. Return the rice to the pot with the 2 teaspoons of flaky sea salt and mix it in, then add about 500ml stock. It may bubble up and steam, so be a little careful. Stir the rice until all of the stock is absorbed, then add another 500ml of stock and stir this in. Turn the heat down to a simmer.

Cut the chard stalks from the leaves and slice the stalks into pieces 5mm thick, then mix these into the risotto. Roll the leaves into a tight bunch and shred them.

Add the thyme and shredded chard leaves to the risotto and again add some stock. The key with risotto is to add stock as required — never letting it sink below the level of the rice, but never drowning it either. Keep adding stock and stirring the risotto until the rice is al dente. When it is, add the mascarpone and keep simmering. The rice will take about 20–28 minutes to cook, so keep tasting a few grains after 20 minutes to reach the desired texture — I like mine with just a little bite to it.

When it's ready, mix in the oregano and half the Parmesan, then take off the heat and cover tightly. Leave to rest for 5 minutes, then mix in a few tablespoons of stock and the extra-virgin olive oil, taste and adjust the seasoning, if necessary.

To serve, spoon into bowls and scatter with the remaining Parmesan.

staples & sides

Four ways with potatoes

The potato must be the West's favourite comfort food – it's certainly mine, along with bread and rice. There are so many varieties of potato, with more arriving on the shelves all the time. Look out for heirloom varieties, which come in different and surprising colours and shapes. Potatoes are basically one of two types: floury or waxy. The former is great for frying and baking, and the latter for salads. Both are good for gratins. As we cook potatoes so often to accompany our meals, it is good to come up with interesting and unusual ways of preparing them to ring the changes. My suggestions here will all serve 4 as a side dish.

Chorizo mash   *top left*

This is really great with grilled fish, sautéed garlic snails or on it's own with purple sprouting broccoli as a starter. You'll need to find cooking chorizo – pork mixed with *pimentón* (smoked paprika) and spices. Peel 500g floury potatoes and boil in lightly salted water. Peel the skin from 250g cooking chorizo and blitz in a food processor to a coarse mince. Place in a pan with 100ml olive oil and cook, stirring continuously, until aromatic and sizzling, about 4 minutes. Mash the potatoes and mix in the chorizo. Adjust the seasoning, if necessary.

Herb-and-cumin roasted chunks   *top right*

These are good served with the Sunday roast, alongside a spicy tomato sauce as a snack, or with roast field mushrooms and spinach as an autumnal lunch. Preheat the oven to 180°C/gas 4. For 4 people, scrub the skins of 500g medium potatoes and cut each into 6 wedges. Cover with cold water and boil for 4 minutes. Drain and place on a baking tray lined with parchment. Scatter with 2–3 tablespoons chopped fresh herbs (try sage, rosemary and thyme) and ½ teaspoon cumin seeds, and season generously. Drizzle with 2–3 tablespoons extra-virgin olive oil and bake until golden and cooked through.

Sautéed minted garlic chips   *bottom right*

These thick chips are lovely served as a snack or as part of a larger meal. Scrub the skins or peel 500g medium waxy potatoes, then slice into 5mm thick discs. Pour 3cm of olive oil into a sauté pan and add a crushed unpeeled garlic clove. Put on a gentle heat and cook until the garlic begins to go golden. Turn the heat up (you want it at 180°C) and add one-quarter of the potatoes. Gently move them around and turn them over once they've gone golden too, and cook until you can insert a knife into them. Remove them once done, together with the garlic. Cook the rest in the same way. As you bring them out of the hot oil, toss with a handful of shredded mint and basil, and serve with a lemon wedge and flaky salt.

Baby potato, dill and red onion salad   *bottom left*

This lovely salad is perfect with oily fish like mackerel and salmon, as well as poached chicken and roast leg of lamb. Boil 500g baby waxy potatoes in lightly salted water until cooked. Meanwhile, slice 1 red onion into thin rings and toss with 4 tablespoons white vinegar (cider or rice vinegar works well) and leave to 'cure'. Drain the potatoes once cooked, then slice them in half lengthways while still hot (use a pair of tongs for this) and put in a bowl. Drain the vinegar from the onions and pour it over the hot potatoes, season generously with freshly ground pepper and salt, add 4 tablespoons extra-virgin olive oil and mix together. Leave to cool, then mix in the onion rings and a small handful of snipped dill.

Four ways with roots

We tend to think of roots as being just potatoes, carrots and parsnips – but there's a huge array of them out there. Many come to us from other culinary cultures, but you can be sure that they're being eaten around the world all the time. The rule-of-thumb with roots is always to put them in plenty of cold water and bring them to the boil – although if you're cutting them up into smaller pieces, cooking them in already boiling water is fine. All roots need to be firm and dense; if they feel fluffy or have any discoloration or rotten bits, avoid them. They store well out of the fridge in a cool, dark and dry place – avoid warmth and light.

If you want to try some slightly more adventurous roots, here are four recipes, most of which will work for almost any type of similar vegetable. All serve 4 as a side dish.

Roast kumara *top left*

Kumara is the native sweet potato of New Zealand. Regular sweet potatoes also work well cooked in this way. Preheat the oven to 180°C/gas 4. Gently scrub the skins of 2–3 kumara (about 600g), then chop off both ends. Cut into 1.5 cm thick discs and boil in salted water for 12 minutes. Drain and sit on a parchment-lined baking tray, drizzle with 4 tablespoons avocado (or extra-virgin olive) oil, season generously and roast until golden and cooked through, about 20 minutes, turning halfway through. Serve as roast potatoes – but they also go really well with any hot fish dish or roast duck.

Salsify *top right*

This is a simple way of serving this undervalued and tasty vegetable. Cut a lemon into quarters and squeeze the juice into a pan, then add the lemon quarters and a litre of cold water. Peel 600g salsify (see page 65) and add to the pan, cutting them to fit the pan if needs be. Bring to the boil, add a large teaspoon of salt and cook until you can just insert a knife through them. Drain, reserving one lemon quarter. Cut the salsify into 1–2cm rounds. Chop the reserved lemon into pieces. Put the pan back on the heat and add 50g butter and 1/2 teaspoon caraway or cumin seeds, and cook over moderate heat until the butter goes nut-brown. Add the salsify and lemon and cook for 3–4 minutes, stirring often, to colour. Season and serve. Serve with poached white meats, steamed fish and roast lamb.

Buttered parsnips *bottom left*

Butter and parsnips are a match made in culinary heaven. Preheat the oven to 180°C/gas 4. Peel 2–3 parsnips, discard top and bottom, and cut across in half, then lengthways into wedges. Grease a 1 litre roasting dish with 80g butter and lay the parsnips in it. Add a few sprigs of thyme, season well and pour in a cup of boiling water. Seal tightly with foil and bake for 45 minutes. Take the foil off and continue to cook until the parsnips are golden. These are particularly good served with roast meat, red and white.

Cassava chips *bottom right*

Always boil this tropical root, also known as yucca, uncovered as it contains traces of toxins that need to be driven off with the steam. These won't harm you, but, like the potato, cassavas contain negligible amounts of chemicals better not eaten in large quantities. Cut 800g cassava into 10cm lengths, then pare off the peel (usually wax-coated to preserve it). Cut each into quarters lengthways and remove the core, then cut the quarters into wedges. Put in a large pot of cold water and bring to the boil, adding a few teaspoons of salt once boiling. Cook until a knife passes easily through it (undercooked cassava is chewy). Drain and lay on a tray to cool, then place in the fridge, uncovered, for 2–4 hours to dry out. Deep-fry a handful at a time in vegetable oil preheated to 180°C until golden and eat like chips.

Creamy peas, shallots and mint _top left_

This is a really simple way to serve peas and make them seem quite lush. Sauté 3 banana shallots (or 6 regular ones) in 2 tablespoons olive oil until softened and beginning to colour. Add 200ml double cream, 100ml water and 400g frozen or fresh peas. Bring to a boil, then simmer rapidly, with a lid fitted loosely to the pan, until the peas are cooked. Season, then add a handful of shredded fresh mint.

Salted edamame _top right_

These tasty crunchy beans (fresh soya beans in the pod) make a great snack to have with a cold beer. The hardest, but not impossible, part will be finding them (try Chinatown or a Japanese food store). Simply bring a large pan of lightly salted water to the boil, add a handful of pods per person and boil for 4 minutes if frozen, 3½ if not. Drain, toss with lots of flaky salt or soy sauce and eat. The trick is to put the pod in your mouth and pull it out, using your teeth to keep back the beans. You can also pod them, once cooked, as you would broad beans, and toss in a pasta dish or salad.

Baby gem and peas _bottom right_

I love this dish – it's such a great combination of textures and green tones. Serve it with some roast racks of spring lamb or slow-cooked shoulder of mutton. Sauté 1 sliced leek in 100g butter with 2 teaspoons fresh thyme leaves in a wide pan until the leek is beginning to caramelize, stirring often. Meanwhile, remove any scraggy outer leaves from 4 baby gem lettuces, trim the stalk ends and cut in half lengthways. Place the lettuce halves in the pan, cut sides facing down, and sauté for another minute. Spoon 250g fresh or frozen peas around and between the lettuce halves, season well, then add 120ml boiling water and cover. Bring to the boil, then simmer for 10 minutes, at which point the peas will be cooked and the lettuce stems should be tender.

Broad beans, red onion and pancetta _bottom left_

This dish is an old favourite and can be made in summer with fresh broad beans and equally as well in the depths of winter using frozen ones. If you can't get pancetta, then use thickly sliced smoked bacon. Fry 100g diced pancetta, 1 thinly sliced red onion and 2 bay leaves, halved lengthways, in 2 tablespoons olive oil in a deepish pan. Cook until the pancetta is beginning to crisp up and the onions caramelize. Add a dozen sage leaves, 400g broad beans and 120ml boiling water. Cover and bring to the boil, then turn down to a rapid simmer and cook until the beans are done, around 10 minutes. Season and add a handful of roughly chopped parsley.

Four ways with peas and pods

The best thing about peas and pods is hulling them – it's a lovely job to do with friends. The next best thing is eating them. Podded vegetables always add a lovely colour to the table and they can be cooked in so many ways. If you're in a dilemma over whether to buy fresh peas or frozen ones then, unless you know the fresh ones are less than a day old, I'd recommend you buy frozen – they'll be sweeter, as they're generally frozen within hours of being picked.

Peas and pods deserve so much more than simple boiling. Try the imaginative treatments I suggest here. All will serve 4 as a side dish.

Four ways with greens

While we tend to lump all 'greens' into one category, they actually belong to a large group made up of quite different characters. We like our greens crunchy and brightly coloured these days, but I've included a couple of recipes for slow-cooked greens – the flavour's still there but the texture changes. It was overcooked Brussels sprouts in my childhood that put me off greens, so you do need to know how to handle them. If you favour boiling, always add them to plenty of rapidly boiling water, putting in the salt just before the greens. Also, don't cover the pan if you want to keep a good colour. Steaming is another, quicker way to cook greens. The rule-of-thumb when buying greens is that they should be firm and plump. If you want to do something slightly more exotic with greens, here are four new ways to try. All will serve 4 as a side dish.

Slow-cooked beans and shiitake mushrooms top left

For a deliciously unusual way with green (or runner and yellow, as here) beans, so they are soft and tender – not crunchy – slice 6 shallots into thin rings and sauté in 2 tablespoons extra-virgin olive oil until wilted. Add 10 shiitake mushrooms, stems removed and caps quartered, and cook for another 2 minutes, stirring twice. Add 300g assorted beans, toss well to coat, then pour in 350ml boiling water. Cover and cook over moderate heat until all the water has evaporated. Season well and serve. These are particularly good served with roast red meats and poultry stews.

Lemon braised Swiss chard top right

I love Swiss chard – and, with the stalk and leaves treated separately, it makes a good staple. Cut the leaves from the stalks of 600g Swiss chard, then cut the stalks into chunks, about 1x4cm. Heat a sauté pan and add 3 tablespoons extra-virgin olive oil, 2 sliced garlic cloves and 1 teaspoon coarsely chopped lemon zest. Fry until coloured, then add the chard stalks and mix together. Cover and cook over a low heat for 5 minutes. Add 2 tablespoons lemon juice and continue to cook until the chard stalks are soft, about 15 minutes. Meanwhile, bring a pot of water to the boil, salt it and add the chard leaves. Bring back to the boil and cook for 4 minutes, then drain. Either purée in a food processor or chop them finely, and then mix into the stalks. Season to taste. Serve with roast lamb and beef.

Spicy sesame wok-fried Brussels sprouts bottom right

For those of you, like me, who are not particularly fond of sprouts, this idea will change your mind. Heat a wok and add 1 tablespoon vegetable oil, followed by 4 chopped garlic cloves, a thumb of ginger, peeled and chopped, and 1 red chilli, chopped (more or less to taste). Fry until beginning to colour. Add 1 teaspoon chopped fresh lemon grass (don't use the outer 2 layers or the base of the stem) and cook for 20 seconds, then add 2 handfuls of Brussels sprouts, sliced into rings. Turn the heat up and add 2 teaspoons toasted sesame seeds (I used a mixture of white and black) and 1 teaspoon toasted sesame oil. Stir over a high heat to cook – you still want them to be crunchy. Add 2 tablespoons soy sauce and toss together, then taste and add extra salt or soy sauce, if necessary. These are especially good served with grilled or steamed fish, poached chicken and barbecued pork chops.

Courgettes, basil and pine nuts bottom left

This is a lovely simple summer dish. Heat a pan and add 1 tablespoon avocado oil (or use olive oil) and 2 tablespoons pine nuts. Once they start to colour, add 3–4 courgettes, trimmed and sliced into discs. Mix well and stir in 4 tablespoons hot water, then season well. Cover and cook until all the water has gone, then mix in a handful of torn basil leaves. These are very good served with steamed white meat and fish.

Four ways with purées

Puréed vegetables needn't just be for babies or the elderly! A good tasty purée makes a lovely bed on which you can rest grilled or pan-fried fish, sliced duck and chicken, roast beef and venison. Purées are often made way too creamy for my palate, masking the flavour of the vegetables themselves. I'd rather let the ingredients speak for themselves. All the recipes here will serve 4 as a side dish.

Carrot, swede and savoy cabbage   top left

This is lovely with a roast or reheated next day in a frying pan and topped with grilled smoked bacon. For 6–8 people, peel and chop 1 large carrot and 1 swede, and put in a large pot with a tablespoon of fresh rosemary. Bring to the boil, add a little salt and cook until you can almost insert a knife through the swede. Add ½ savoy cabbage, thinly sliced, and cook for 5 minutes more. Strain and pulse in a food processor with 4 tablespoons extra-virgin olive oil or 80g butter to a coarse texture. Taste and season.

Baba ganoush   top centre

This is delicious as a dip with warm pita bread, or with a chunk of grilled fish on top, but it's also a winner on wholewheat toast with tomatoes. For 4 people, turn a gas burner on, sit a large aubergine across it and cook, turning frequently (turn extractor on full), until quite soft. It'll look terribly burnt, but the smoky taste you get is priceless. If you don't have a gas burner, you can grill it or roast it in a very hot oven – but do PRICK IT several times before doing this – they can pop open and burn you if you're not careful. Once cooked, split it lengthways, keeping the stalk end intact, and sit it in a colander or sieve to drain and cool (you'll be surprised how much liquid comes out). Peel off the skin; some will stick but do your best and gently rinse it to remove any burnt pieces. Discard the stalk end and chop into a coarse pulp, then mix with 2 heaped tablespoons tahini, 150ml thick plain Greek-style yoghurt and 3 tablespoons lemon juice. Season.

Celeriac and red cabbage   top right

This pink-purple purée is really earthy-tasting – which belies its rather camp appearance. It is great served with red meats and hearty fish like poached salt cod and grilled grey mullet. For 6 people, peel 1 medium celeriac and cut it into even-sized chunks. Cook in boiling salted water with a bay leaf, 2 sliced garlic cloves and a few sprigs of thyme until you can almost insert a knife through it. Add ¼ red cabbage and boil for a further 8 minutes. Strain, discard the herbs and put in a food processor (or use a mouli) with 150g butter. Make a smooth purée and then season it.

Sweet potato, ginger and chilli   bottom right

This goes really well with duck, pork and chicken – the sweetness of the potatoes complements these meats. It's also lovely with roast pumpkin and field mushrooms. For 4–6 people, peel and dice 2 sweet potatoes and put in a pot of cold water with ½ sliced red chilli (with the seeds), a thumb of peeled and thinly sliced ginger and 2 teaspoons fine salt. Bring to the boil, then simmer with the lid on until cooked. Drain in a colander and tip into a food processor. Add 1 teaspoon toasted sesame seeds and 2 teaspoons toasted sesame oil, and blitz. The potato should become fine, but you want the chillies and ginger to retain some texture. Taste and season.

pickles & preserves

Saffron-pickled lotus root

These and the Dill and Mustard Pickled Cucumber on page 140 are what I call 'fridge pickles'. You can't leave them on the shelf in the pantry – they need to be stored in the fridge. They'll last for up to 8 weeks, if kept covered with pickling liquid and tightly sealed, even after you have used some of them. The premise of these pickles is much the same – approximately one part of vinegar to two parts of water, with seasoning, sweetness and flavourings to taste. These lotus root pickles are lovely when used to garnish a main course, such as grilled fish or roast chicken, or a vegetable pasta or rice dish. They're great added to both warm and cold salads, put on top of cheese on toast after it's been grilled or just snacked on after a meal, as the Japanese do with pickles.

makes one 1 litre jar

350g lotus root

250ml rice wine vinegar (or use cider or white wine vinegar)

1 thumb of ginger, peeled and cut into fine julienne strips

2 good pinches of saffron

2 teaspoons salt

3 tablespoons runny honey

Peel the lotus root and cut it into slices about 2mm thick (using a mandolin grater is best for this). Place in a large bowl of cold water and rinse thoroughly, then leave a gentle flow of cold water running through it while you prepare the rest.

Place everything else in a pan with 450ml water and bring to the boil. Fill a heatproof preserving jar with boiling water and leave to sit for a minute on a folded tea towel (it helps, trust me). Tip the hot water from the jar, drain the lotus root slices and place in the jar, then pour as much of the boiling liquid over them as you can, adding as much of the ginger as possible, and seal while hot. If you are recycling a jar, it is important to use a new seal or a very tight-fitting lid. Leave to cool on the tea towel, then place in the fridge. Leave for at least 3 days before using.

Aunty Mary's chow chow

My aunty Mary, much like my paternal grandmother Molly, is an expert chutney and relish maker, and this is her recipe. In my home in New Zealand, piccalilli was called chow chow and we used to eat this with cheese and cold meats.

Makes about 3kg or 3 one litre jars

1 medium cauliflower (about 400g), separated into florets

200g beans, trimmed and halved

8–10 green or unripe red tomatoes, cut into eighths

1 cucumber (about 300g), cut lengthways, then into chunks

6 white onions, thickly sliced

110g fine table salt

750ml cider vinegar or white wine vinegar

600g white sugar

3 tablespoons mustard seeds

1 teaspoon coarsely ground black pepper

5 tablespoons flour

1 heaped tablespoon turmeric

1 heaped tablespoon mustard powder

In a large non-reactive bowl, mix the veg with the salt and leave for 5 minutes. Then pour on enough cold water to submerge everything (although the veg will begin to float) and mix well. Cover and leave to cure for 24 hours in a cool place away from sunlight, mixing twice.

Next day, drain in a colander. Have your jars sterilized and filled with hot water. In a large pot, put all but 200ml of the vinegar, together with the sugar, mustard seeds and pepper. Add the drained vegetables and bring to the boil, stirring often. Cook at a rapid simmer until the cauliflower is almost done (around 5–8 minutes) – you still want it to have a little crunch.

Dissolve the flour, turmeric and mustard powder in the remaining vinegar, then mix this into the vegetables, stirring thoroughly to avoid lumps. Bring to the boil and cook for a further 30 seconds, gently stirring all the time.

Decant into the drained jars and seal while warm. Sit on a tray lined with a tea towel and leave to cool. Store in the fridge and use within 4 months.

Pickled red cabbage and gooseberries

This pickle goes really well with oily fish like salmon and mackerel, or it makes a delicious salad tossed with sliced apples or pears, toasted hazelnuts and olive oil. Make it at least a week before you want to use it, and keep it in the fridge.

makes three 1 litre jars

700ml red wine vinegar or cider vinegar

500g white sugar

1 teaspoon ground cloves

1 medium red cabbage (about 900g), core removed and finely shredded

400g gooseberries (both green and red are delicious)

Have your jars sterilized and filled with hot water. Place the vinegar, sugar and cloves in a pan with 850ml water and 2½ teaspoons fine salt, then bring to the boil.

Drain the jars of hot water and lay in a roasting dish lined with a thick kitchen cloth. Divide the cabbage and gooseberries among the jars in layers (I like to start and finish with gooseberries), packing them in tightly.

Carefully pour the boiling pickling liquid into the jars, poking the cabbage gently with the handle of a wooden spoon to loosen air bubbles. There should be more liquid than you need – let the excess drizzle out of the jars. Make sure there is nothing trapped on the lip of the jars and seal while hot.

Once cool, flip the jars over and leave for 24 hours. Rinse the jars and store in the fridge. Use within 4 months and within 12 days of opening.

Pickled wild mushrooms

serves 6–8 as an accompaniment

4 garlic cloves, roughly chopped

½ teaspoon cracked black pepper

4 tablespoons extra-virgin olive oil

10 stems of thyme (or try oregano, or half the amount of rosemary)

250ml white vinegar (try cider, rice or white wine vinegar)

2 teaspoons flaky salt

500g mushrooms, cleaned as on the right

Wild mushrooms come in a huge range of varieties, and they can be quite seasonal. To make this pickle really interesting, however, get a selection of at least three different types available at the time. Make sure there are no twigs or insects among them, and gentle brushing with a dry pastry brush will help dislodge the grit that invariably clings to wild foods. If the mushrooms are very dirty, then you can wash them as a last resort, but handle them gently and drain them as quickly and pat them as dry as you can once you've gently sloshed them in a bowl of tepid water. If you have a selection of large and small mushrooms, then cut the large ones into quarters. These pickled mushrooms are great served sprinkled on salads and spooned over pasta or risottos, or alongside roast meats and grilled fish.

In a large pan, fry the garlic and black pepper in the olive oil until the garlic is just beyond golden. Add the thyme and fry for 30 seconds, then add the vinegar and 500ml cold water. Bring to the boil, then add the salt and mushrooms and bring back to the boil, gently stirring the mushrooms so that they cook evenly. Once everything has come to the boil, remove from the heat, cover and leave to cool.

Transfer the mushrooms to a dish or jar and place, covered, in the fridge. Leave them there for at least a day before using them, and for up to 5 days.

Dill and mustard pickled cucumber

Similar to the 'fridge pickles' on pages 134–6, these are great with cold potato salad, with pickled herrings and sardines, or eaten as a snack or in a cheese sandwich.

makes one 1 litre jar

250ml white wine vinegar (or cider or rice vinegar)

2 teaspoons salt

4 tablespoons caster sugar

1 large cucumber

4 banana shallots (or 8 ordinary shallots)

4 garlic cloves, sliced

1 teaspoon coarsely ground black pepper

3 tablespoons mustard seeds

2 small handfuls of dill, chopped roughly into 2cm lengths

a few sprigs of oregano

Place the vinegar, salt and caster sugar in a pan with 450ml water and bring to the boil.

Fill a heatproof jar with boiling water and leave to sit for a minute on a folded tea towel.

Cut both ends from the cucumber and slice it quite thinly, then place the slices in a bowl.

Peel and slice the shallots, then add to the cucumber, together with the garlic, pepper, mustard seeds, dill and oregano.

Drain the hot water from the jar and pack it with the cucumber mixture. Pour the boiling pickling liquid over the cucumber and seal the jar while hot. Leave to cool on the tea towel, then place in the fridge. Leave for at least 3 days before using.

Oven-dried tomatoes in olive oil

These give you a similar result to sun-blushed tomatoes, but they're much less sweet and they're a good way of using an excess of tomatoes. Try serving them tossed through pasta, in salads, with cheese, and even chopped and added to a simple risotto.

makes one 500ml jar

500g plum tomatoes

2 bay leaves

100ml extra-virgin olive oil, plus more for topping up the jar

Preheat the oven to 120°C/gas ½ and line a roasting dish with baking parchment.

Cut the tomatoes across in half and scoop out and discard the seeds. Cut each half across again in half. Place the bay leaves in the dish and sit the tomatoes in it. Drizzle with the 100ml olive oil, season generously with salt and pepper, then place in the centre of the oven and cook for 1 ½–2 hours. You don't want the tomatoes to colour at all, but to dry out a bit. They must still look a little plump, though, and not at all desiccated.

Heat a jar in the oven for 10 minutes with the tomatoes (removing any rubber seals), then place the tomatoes and bay leaves in the jar, pour in the cooking oil and juices, and top up with extra olive oil to the jar's lip.

Seal and leave to cool at room temperature, then store in the fridge for up to 8 weeks. The tomatoes will be fine if kept covered with the oil. The oil may solidify when it is kept in the fridge, giving it a spotty look, but it will be fine if allowed to warm to room temperature.

Aubergine, cumin, coriander and mint relish

This relish is absolutely fantastic served with roast lamb, grilled oily fish or a vegetable curry. It can also be tossed through pasta and dredged with lots of pecorino or Parmesan.

serves 6–8 as an accompaniment

vegetable oil for deep-frying

1 aubergine, cut into 2cm chunks

1 red onion, thinly sliced

grated zest of 1 lime and the juice of 2

3 tablespoons lemon juice

1 tablespoon cumin seeds

2 tablespoons extra-virgin olive oil

1 teaspoon flaky salt

large handful of mint, leaves separated and stems discarded

large handful of coriander, leaves separated and stems cut into 1cm pieces

1 spring onion, thinly sliced

Heat 6cm vegetable cooking oil to 180°C and fry the aubergine in 3–4 batches until golden brown. Drain well on absorbent kitchen paper set on a wide tray and leave to cool.

Mix the onion with the lime and lemon juices and the lime zest. Leave for at least 30 minutes, mixing often – the onions should become more pinky-red as they macerate.

In a small frying pan, fry the cumin seeds with 1 teaspoon of the olive oil until golden, then tip on top of the onions, together with the remaining olive oil and flaky salt. Mix in the aubergine, herbs and spring onion. Leave to allow the flavours to develop for at least an hour and eat within 24 hours. Keep covered in the fridge and mix before serving.

Beetroot-pickled beansprouts

These are really good served on top of steamed new potatoes, tossed into salads, scattered on soup, or mixed with coriander and spring onions as a garnish for roast salmon and other oily fish.

makes one 1 litre jar

1 large beetroot, peeled

2 garlic cloves, chopped

200ml cider vinegar (or white wine or rice vinegar)

6 tablespoons caster sugar

350g beansprouts, rinsed and drained

12 allspice berries

Either grate the beetroot or purée it in a small food processor. Place in a pot with the garlic, vinegar, sugar and 400ml water. Bring to the boil, then simmer rapidly for 5 minutes.

Meanwhile, fill a heatproof jar with boiling water and leave to sit for a minute on a folded tea towel. Tip the hot water from the jar, then place the beansprouts and allspice in the jar, layering them.

Strain the hot pickling liquid through a fine sieve, then pour as much of it as you can over the sprouts in the jar and seal while hot. Leave to cool on the tea towel, then place in the fridge. Leave for at least a day before using.

desserts

2 large handfuls of seedless red grapes, stalks removed

4 tablespoons pomegranate molasses

1 celeriac root, peeled and cut into 8 chunks

6 tablespoons unrefined caster sugar

pared rind and juice of 1 lemon

butter or vegetable oil for frying the fritters

100ml crème fraîche

for the fritter mixture

1½ tablespoons polenta grains

2 tablespoons flour

1 teaspoon baking powder

1 egg

½ teaspoon pure vanilla extract

2 tablespoons thick yoghurt

Celeriac and ginger fritters with pomegranate roast grapes

I like these fritters because they're not too sweet, and celeriac gives such an unexpected flavour – not one usually associated with a dessert. You can add various spices to the mixture, like ground cloves and nutmeg, star anise or allspice. These roast grapes are served at The Providores in both sweet and savoury dishes (in a tea-smoked salmon and baby gem salad) and will keep in the fridge for up to a week. The fritters are also delicious served with roast peaches or poached stone fruit and vanilla ice cream.

Preheat the oven to 180°C/gas 4. Put the grapes in a roasting dish, preferably ceramic, that will just hold them in a single layer. Drizzle with the pomegranate molasses and add 2 tablespoons of water. Bake in the oven for 20–30 minutes, until they've given off some juice and have begun to look a little shrivelled.

While they cook, place the celeriac in a pot with 4 tablespoons of the sugar, a pinch of salt and the lemon rind and juice. Barely cover with cold water, cover and cook until just tender – a knife should just go through it. Drain, discarding the lemon rind, and leave to cool in a colander.

Make the fritter mixture: sieve the polenta, flour and baking powder. Once the celeriac has cooled, grate it coarsely and place in a bowl with the remaining sugar, the egg, vanilla and yoghurt, and mix together. Mix in the sieved mixture and leave to rest for 20 minutes.

Heat a pan, preferably non-stick, and add a little butter or oil. Cook spoonfuls of the mixture, making sure you don't overcrowd the pan. You can make them as large or small as you want. Flip them over once golden and cook on the other side – they'll need about 4–5 minutes in total. If they colour too quickly, your pan is too hot. They are best eaten warm, so keep any cooked ones in a low oven while you finish all of the mixture.

To serve, place one or two fritters (depending on their size) on a plate and dollop on some crème fraîche, then spoon the grapes and their juice on the plates.

Beetroot and chocolate mousse cake

This flourless, eggless mousse cake is a real oddity in that it tastes both sweet and slightly savoury, and it seems to alternate flavours of chocolate and beetroot on the tongue. It can be made vegan by using some of the really good sugar- and dairy-free chocolate available (my favourite is from Rococo) but, funnily enough, it's delicious served with whipped cream! If you can't get hold of really dark chocolate, then use the darkest you can find and add a few tablespoons of dark cocoa – it really makes it that much richer.

Makes one large 24cm cake (enough to feed 10–12)

375g roasted and peeled beetroot, cut into chunks

450g firm silken tofu (a Japanese Tetra Pak works well, available from health-food stores)

70g unrefined caster sugar

1 tablespoon vanilla extract

1 teaspoon baking powder

350g chocolate (minimum 60% cocoa solids), melted

chocolate shards or fruit and cream to serve (optional)

Preheat the oven to 180°C/gas 4 and line the base and sides of a 24cm loose-bottomed round cake tin with baking parchment – but don't grease it.

Place the beetroot, tofu, sugar, vanilla and baking powder in a food processor and blitz to a fine purée. Tip into a bowl and mix in the melted chocolate.

Pour into the tin and bake for 30 minutes. The cake will look quite uncooked but don't panic – it will be fine. Leave to cool completely (it's quite a soft cake), then remove from the tin and place on a large plate. Store in the fridge until needed, but bring back to room temperature before you want to eat it.

To serve, simply cut into wedges and decorate with chocolate shards or serve with fruit (it's great with berries, pineapple and mango) and, if you like, cream.

Pumpkin pie with meringue topping

This must be the most common vegetable dessert. You'll find it throughout the USA and, as a kid growing up in New Zealand, I would make it often. It's also great baked in a pie dish with a biscuit-crumb base in place of the pastry. If you can't get pumpkin, you can use butternut squash successfully, and kumara and firm sweet potatoes also work surprisingly well. If you want to serve this as a cold dessert, you need to be aware that the meringue will collapse if left for too long. So, it's better to make the pie(s) up to the stage where you have baked the filling, but then let them cool. Just before serving, whisk up the meringue as described and bake.

300g shortcrust pastry

300g pumpkin, peeled and deseeded, flesh cut into chunks

125ml double cream

4 tablespoons caster sugar

$\frac{1}{2}$ teaspoon ground allspice

$\frac{1}{2}$ teaspoon five-spice powder

2 eggs, separated

4 drops of pure vanilla extract

4 tablespoons icing sugar

runny cream or vanilla ice cream, to serve

Roll out the pastry on a lightly floured surface and use to line four 10cm loose-bottomed tart pans or one 24cm pan. Chill for 30 minutes.

Preheat the oven to 180°C/gas 4. Line the tart shell(s) with baking parchment, weight with baking beans or dried pulses and blind-bake until just golden brown (12–15 minutes). Remove from the oven, then remove the beans and lining paper.

While the pastry is being prepared, place the pumpkin and a pinch of salt in a medium-sized pan and cover with cold water. Cover with a lid and boil until just cooked.

Once the pumpkin is cooked, drain off the cooking water and add the cream, sugar and spices. Mash together over the heat until it comes to a gloopy boil. Take off the heat and whisk in the egg yolks and vanilla. Tip the mixture into the tart shell(s) and bake in the oven until the mixture sets. As the mix is already quite hot, it should only take 8–10 minutes. It's ready when it feels firm to the touch.

While the mix is baking, whisk the egg whites with the icing sugar until fluffy and glossy. Then spread this on the top of the pie(s), covering the crust. Turn the oven-grill to medium and place the pies on a baking tray about 15cm under it. Keep the door ajar and bake until the meringue colours golden. Take from the oven and carefully remove the pie(s) from the tin(s). Serve with runny cream or vanilla ice cream.

makes one 20–24cm round cake or 15 cupcakes

180g unsalted butter, plus more for greasing

200g flour, plus more for dusting

160g plus 2 tablespoons unrefined caster sugar

5 tablespoons runny honey

3 eggs, lightly beaten

2 pinches of salt

½ teaspoon baking soda

1½ teaspoons baking powder

¼ teaspoon ground turmeric

1 teaspoon sweet spice of choice (cinnamon, nutmeg, ginger)

150g carrot, peeled and grated

100g sweetcorn kernels, cut from 1 corn cob

60g chopped unpeeled almonds, lightly toasted

300g pineapple (about ½ a large one), peeled and core removed

for the minted topping

1 tablespoon unrefined caster sugar

small handful of mint leaves

120g cream cheese

5 tablespoons double cream

Carrot, almond and sweetcorn cake with minted cream cheese and pineapple

The addition of sweetcorn in this cake gives it both an unexpected flavour and a lovely texture. If you can't get fresh sweetcorn, use canned corn – just make sure it's not flavoured with peppers or herbs. Replacing the mint in the topping with basil gives a surprise as well.

Preheat the oven to 180˚C/gas 4 and prepare a 20–24cm round cake tin or 15 muffin tins by buttering and flouring them, or spray them with baking oil.

In a mixing bowl, cream the butter, the 160g sugar and all the honey, then add the beaten egg in 4 batches – the mix will sometimes look curdled, but don't worry – it will be fine.

Sift the 200g flour, salt, baking soda and baking powder, and the spices, and slowly mix these in. Then mix in the carrot, corn and almonds.

Spoon the mixture into the prepared cake tin or muffin tins and bake for 20–40 minutes – the cake taking longer to cook. It's done when a skewer inserted into the thickest part comes out clean. Leave to cool for 10 minutes before turning out.

While the cake is cooking, cut the pineapple into small dice and mix with the remaining 2 tablespoons of sugar. Lay the dice on baking parchment on a baking tray and bake with the cake until they begin to caramelize, about 15 minutes. Then remove from the oven.

To make the minted topping, pound the sugar with the mint leaves, then beat this mixture into the cream cheese and cream, forming firm peaks.

To serve, spread the minted topping over the cooled cake or muffins and top with the pineapple.

Kumara and rosemary brioche with maple syrup-poached pear

If you can't get hold of kumara – New Zealand's sweet potato – you can use regular sweet potatoes or potatoes, but, as they all have differing moisture content, you may need to add a little extra flour. The vanilla pod is baked in the dough for added flavour. The pears are rich from the maple syrup and any left over are great mixed into porridge for a warming breakfast. They can be prepared up to 5 days in advance, if kept stored in the fridge in their cooking liquor.

serves 6 (although the brioche will be enough for 20 slices)

200g peeled kumara, thinly sliced

250ml milk, plus more for brushing

1 vanilla pod, split in half and quartered

1 cinnamon stick, snapped in half

1 level teaspoon fresh or dried yeast

300g strong flour or more as necessary

60g muscovado sugar

1½ teaspoons chopped fresh rosemary

2 teaspoons orange zest

3 egg yolks

100g unsalted butter, at room temperature

100g mascarpone cheese to serve

for the poached pears

3 pears, peeled, cored and halved lengthways

2 thumbs of ginger, peeled and thinly sliced

200ml maple syrup

6cm stalk of rosemary

The day before, make the brioche (these quantities will make more than you need but it freezes well and lasts for several weeks). Place the kumara, milk, vanilla and cinnamon in a pan and bring to the boil, then simmer until the kumara is cooked. Drain the milk from the pan and pour 150ml of it into a bowl, together with the kumara and vanilla. Discard the cinnamon and remaining milk, then leave to cool to tepid – any hotter and you'll kill the yeast. Add the yeast and mash everything. Leave until the yeast bubbles.

Sift the 300g flour and ¼ teaspoon of salt into a mixing bowl with the sugar, rosemary and orange zest, then add the kumara mix and knead with a dough hook or your hands for 5 minutes until it has all come together. Knead in the egg yolks one at a time until incorporated, then slowly add the butter in 5 batches, until you have a soft dough. If it's very wet, knead in up to a cup of extra flour until no longer sticky. Place in a bowl, cover with cling film and leave in a warm place until it rises. Once increased in size by about a third, knock the air out of it, re-wrap and place in the fridge for 18–24 hours.

Next day, take it from the fridge, punch it a few times, then bring it back to room temperature. When doubled in size, knock it back again, then place in a 1.5 litre loaf tin lined with baking parchment. Cover loosely with cling film and let it rise until doubled in size.

Preheat the oven to 220°C/gas 7. Brush the top of the loaf with a little milk and place in the oven. Quickly and carefully scatter 100ml boiling water over the bottom of the oven (it provides helpful steam) and bake for 15 minutes. Turn the oven down to 180°C/gas 4 and bake for a further 20 minutes. Poke a skewer into the centre of the loaf and it should come out clean. Take from the oven, leave to cool for 30 minutes, then tip out.

To poach the pears, place them in a pan with the ginger, maple syrup and rosemary. Add enough cold water to cover by 1cm, then bring to the boil. Turn to a simmer and cook for 45 minutes, with a cartouche or upturned saucer on top to keep them fully submerged. Let cool in the liquid.

To serve, grill or toast 6 slices of brioche and spread generously with the mascarpone, sit a pear half on top and spoon over some syrup mixture.

index

Acknowledgements

Thanks once again to:

My partner Michael McGrath for allowing me the space at home, and for his ongoing support to get this cooked and written, as well as his tasty comments. Likewise Jeremy Leeming, our partner at The Providores restaurant, for his feedback.

Gareth Balance, my vegetable man, has been fantastic in sourcing vegetables, and the kitchen team at The Providores, led by Miles Kirby and Cris Hossack have been wonderful. As have our partners Annie and Derek Smail, Savas Ertunc and Tarik Bayazit, and my agent Felicity Rubinstein.

The creative team who first came together working on *Salads*: photographer Jean Cazals and I had fun on this, our fifth book together; Lewis Esson edited and cropped a book commissioned by Quadrille's Jane O'Shea; Sue Rowlands provided croissants and lovely props; and the clever Lawrence Morton designed it lovingly.

www.peter-gordon.net